THE COUNTRY HOUSE GARDEN
— *A Grand Tour* —

THE COUNTRY HOUSE GARDEN
A GRAND TOUR

Text by
Gervase Jackson-Stops

Photographs by
James Pipkin

A New York Graphic Society Book
Little, Brown and Company
Boston

First United States Edition

Library of Congress Catalog Card No. 87-61055

First published in the United Kingdom by Pavilion Books Limited

New York Graphic Society books are published by Little, Brown and Company (Inc.).

Printed in Italy

*Frontispiece: The Water Garden at Blenheim Palace, created by Achille Duchêne
for the 9th Duke of Marlborough between 1925 and 1928.*

CONTENTS

PREFACE

The *Treasure Houses of Britain* exhibition held at the National Gallery of Art in Washington in 1985-86 drew attention as never before to the immense cultural significance of the country house. While the catalogue was naturally devoted to its history as a focus of patronage and art-collecting over five centuries, our companion book, *The English Country House – A Grand Tour*, tried to give an idea of its architectural setting, room by room, examining the sequence of state apartments as they developed from the beginning of the Tudor to the end of the Hanoverian periods.

This book is intended to treat the wider garden and landscape setting of the country house in much the same way, examining in turn the different elements to be found on the circuit walk as opposed to the enfilade – marvels of topiary to match the elaborate flying testers of Baroque state beds, lakes and cascades to reflect the silver salvers and wine fountains of the dining-room *buffet*, flower gardens to rival the brilliant hues of crimson and green silk-damask walls.

The importance of the garden as an integral part of the country house has been a recurring theme in art throughout the ages, from the Montacute *millefleurs* tapestry suggesting the 'flowery meads' of the medieval garden, to Sir John Lavery's *Family Group at St Fagan's*, an Edwardian tea party on the terrace, with all the nostalgia of Henry James' *English Hours*. Formal layouts are depicted in Griffier's *View of Syon* and the famous *Presentation of a Pineapple to Charles II*, while Delft tulip vases and flower pieces by Monnoyer helped bring the Baroque garden indoors. Then there are the views of Chiswick by Rysbrack and Lambert showing William Kent's move towards an informal 'Picturesque' style of gardening in the early eighteenth century, followed by landscapes by the Old Masters – Claude, Poussin and Salvator Rosa, Cuyp and Ruysdael – which conditioned the taste of the later 'Natural Landscape' School. Thomas Robins' charming watercolour of Davenport, a design by 'Capability' Brown and one of Repton's 'Red Books' show the progress of this movement towards the *jardin anglais*, while Thomas Daniell's *View of West Wycombe* portrays a house so totally subservient to its setting that its façades were conceived as a series of garden buildings or 'eye-catchers' rather than as an architectural entity – looking forward to the full-blown romanticism of Turner's *Tabley House and Lake: Windy Day*. Even ceramics with the

Chelsea pastoral groups, Hans Sloane botanical plates, and views of famous gardens on Wedgwood and Worcester pieces, underline the country-house owner's passion for horticulture.

Although the gardens illustrated in this book have been carefully picked as archetypes of a particular style or date, it is obviously much rarer to find the 'untouched' here than inside the country house, where decorative schemes of the sixteenth or seventeenth centuries can still be found intact. Gardens are in a constant state of evolution, either decaying through neglect or changing through fashion, the availability of labour and machinery, or even natural conditions. Thus, even in a relatively modern garden like Sissinghurst, which the National Trust is pledged to keep as it was in V. Sackville-West's day, the carpet of polyanthus that was such a striking feature of the nuttery has now impoverished the soil to the point where it has had to be replaced by other plants, giving a very different effect – at least for the time being.

Reconstruction of the gardens of the past can never be wholly accurate. But whether looking at the Elizabethan garden through 1930s spectacles – as at Packwood – or the seventeenth-century Anglo-Dutch garden through 1970s spectacles – as at Westbury – the spirit of the original can be hauntingly evoked, and the old bird's-eye views, the parterres proudly depicted in the backgrounds of ancient family portraits, or the sylvan scenes of faded Mortlake tapestries, can come startlingly to life.

The renewed interest in garden history as an academic discipline has helped to establish greater accuracy in recent years, as can be seen in the restorations of formal layouts like Hatfield and Ham, as much as informal landscapes like Claremont and Painshill. At the same time it has helped to identify many rare features of early garden layouts that still survive even in the unlikely surroundings of a public park – from beds of flowers in the shape of giant baskets, derived from Repton, to the floral clock, so dear to the mayor and corporation, that goes back to the clipped box sundial of the sixteenth century.

This book owes much to the pioneering studies that have appeared in *Garden History* since 1972, and more recently in the *Journal of Garden History*, and to books like Roy Strong's *Renaissance Garden in England*, and Peter Willis and John Dixon Hunt's *Genius of the Place*, with its very useful anthology of writers on the subject between 1620 and 1820. Less space is devoted to planting, always the most ephemeral aspect of gardening, than to more permanent architectural elements like gates and gatepiers, lawns and terraces, statues and urns, canals and cascades. But so many books have appeared on the purely horticultural aspect of the country-house garden in recent years that no apology need be offered for this natural bias.

Once more it has been a pleasure to work with James Pipkin, whose photographs have caught the magic of the British summer despite its notorious unreliability, and whose eye for the unusual viewpoint and the telling detail have never in my experience been equalled. My thanks are also due to the National Trust's Gardens Adviser, John Sales, for much helpful advice, and to Maggie Grieve who brought this book, like its predecessor, to the light of day.

For the rest, I can only echo John Evelyn's letter to Sir Thomas Browne, written in 1657 to explain his projected (but never completed) *Elysium Britannicum*:

'The truth is, that which imported me to discourse on this subject after this sorte, was the many defects which I encounter'd in Bookes and in Gardens, wherein neither words nor cost had bin wanting, but judgement very much; and though I cannot boast of my science in this kind, as both unbecoming my yeares and my small experience, yet I esteem'd it pardonable at least, if in doing my endeavour to rectifie some mistakes, and advancing so usefull and innocent a divertisement, I made some essay, and cast in my Symbole with the rest. To this designe, if forraine observation may conduce, I might likewise hope to refine upon some particulars, especially concerning the ornaments of Gardens, which I shall endeavour so to handle, as that they may become usefull and practicable, as well as magnificent, and that persons of all conditions and faculties, which delight in Gardens, may therein encounter something for their owne advantage.'

Gervase Jackson-Stops

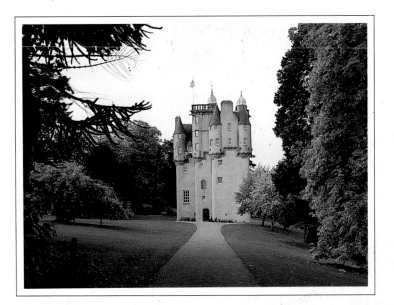

THE HOUSE IN ITS SETTING

'**G**od Almightie first Planted a Garden', the famous opening words of Francis Bacon's essay 'Of Gardens', published in 1625, are a reminder of one of the oldest myths in the history of the world – the natural order represented by the Garden of Eden before the Fall, a place of lost innocence for which men have yearned for many thousands of years. It could be said that the search for the groves of Eden or the pastures of Arcadia, whether Christian or Classical in origin, lies at the very heart of the human psyche. The man-made garden thus has its origins not simply as a utilitarian means of providing food, but as an ideal setting for domestic life, a vision that may have taken very different forms over the centuries, but which has retained its promise, renewed with the buds of each succeeding spring.

The Scottish fortress and its garden: (above) the simple woodland setting of Craigievar, Aberdeenshire; (left) the formal splendour of Drummond Castle, Perthshire.

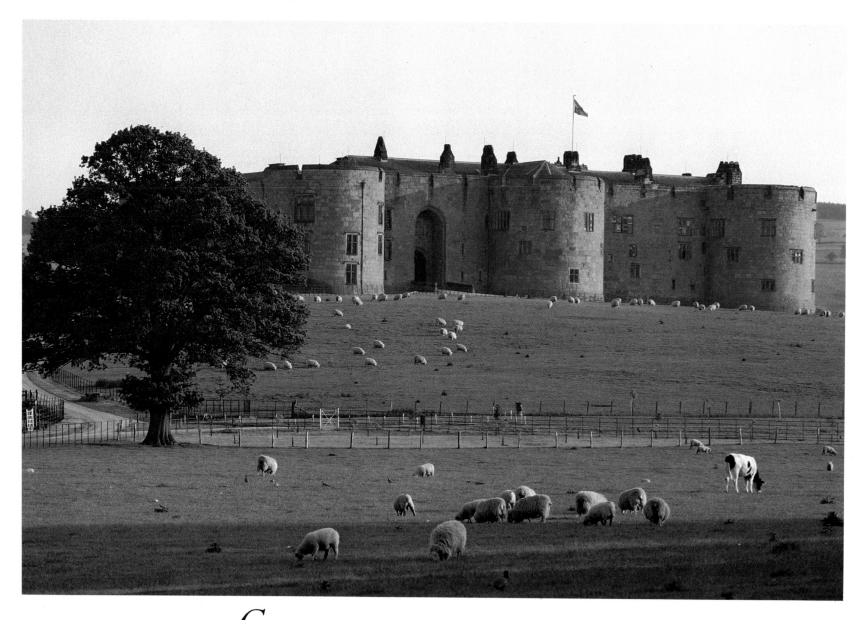

*C*hirk Castle, on the Welsh border, begun in 1295. The elaborate gardens
laid out round it in the seventeenth century were swept away by Capability Brown's
contemporary, William Emes, between 1761 and 1774.

For the Islamic world, the source of so many traditions in European horticulture, the garden was and is a place of enclosure, a walled oasis whose green shade offers a sanctuary from the merciless heat of the surrounding desert. The *hortus conclusus*, whether belonging to the castle or the monastery, followed the same principle, fortified both against hostile nature and against hostile human forces in an age of almost perpetual warfare. Like the stone arcades of the cloister, its tunnel-like arbours surrounding a central lawn planted with pears, cherries and medlars, provided a shady walk in fine weather – especially intended for the ladies of the household, at a time when the separation of the sexes also followed oriental practice. Diminutive gardens of this sort, often with a central wall or fountain, would usually be found within the castle walls, bordered by buildings on two or more sides, and with no relationship to the surrounding landscape.

Until the late sixteenth century, the choice of site for a house would depend almost entirely on how well it could be fortified, or how well it was supplied with water, and gardens appear to have been very much an afterthought. In the north of England and Scotland, where castles were usually built on high ground, the harsh climate encouraged the establishment of walled gardens on south-facing slopes some way away from the house, and this continued to be the normal practice even in the seventeenth and eighteenth centuries.

In the south, where the surroundings were likely to be less rugged, the old idea of the *hortus conclusus* was developed under the Tudors into a series of separate, enclosed gardens closely adjoining the house, whose emblematic tableaux could be 'read' from the windows of the state rooms high up at the top of the building. Slowly, the influence of the Italian Renaissance came to be felt, and with it the idea that, just as man lay at the centre of creation, so his house should be surrounded by gardens forming a miniature cosmos.

Alberti's *De re aedificatoria*, published in 1452 but little known in England till the following century, was of immense importance in gathering together for the first time all the classical references to gardens, including Pliny's famous descriptions of his villas at Tusculum and Laurentum. According to Alberti, the garden should be an extension of the house, expressed by geometrical design, and thus the province of the architect. Perhaps the first English garden to follow these precepts was at Wollaton in Nottinghamshire, built by Robert Smythson for Sir Francis Willoughby in the 1580s, with eight square enclosures laid out round the house, exactly corresponding with it in

Blair Castle in the Scottish Highlands, dominating the wide valley of Glen Tilt.

size. Few other Elizabethan houses were planned as an architectural unit with their gardens, but the relationship between the two was often stressed by the Italianate device of a loggia. At Wimbledon in Surrey and at Castle Ashby in Northamptonshire, these were placed on the side elevation overlooking the 'privy garden', but they could also be on the main garden front, as at Cranborne in Dorset.

The difference between the 'great garden' and the 'privy garden' precisely reflected the difference between the state rooms and the private apartments within the house: the first open to a vast concourse of household attendants, visitors and hangers-on; the second reserved only for the use of the family and the highest-ranking of their guests. At the 'prodigy houses' of great courtiers, like Sir Christopher Hatton's Holdenby, the gardens were also conceived like their counterpart rooms as a setting for masques and entertainments on a huge scale, their precise geometry reflecting the movements of the dances, and their symbolism reinforcing the tributes to Elizabeth I – whether as Astræa, the Virgin Queen, Diana the chaste huntress, or in one of her other allegorical personae.

Powis Castle in North Wales, overlooking William Winde's seventeenth-century terraces.

In the 1630s and '40s the axial geometry of the garden in relation to the house grew stronger. At Wilton, near Salisbury, the revolutionary Palladian architecture of the south front was matched by a garden like those of the Venetian villas on the Brenta, extending the whole width of the house, with a central axial path leading down to the river Avon. Another group of houses, including Little Hadham in Hertfordshire and Sir John Danvers' house in Chelsea, carried this a stage further with the parterre surrounded by raised terraces on all four sides, that opposite the house with an elaborate central staircase and corner pavilions balancing the architectural weight of the main building.

On the whole, the effect of these gardens was static, however, and it was only in the Baroque period that the newly fashionable enfilades, imparting a sense of movement inside the house, found an equivalent in the radiating *allées* and vistas outside. Advances in the understanding of optics were behind this development, just as they influenced the increasingly three-dimensional compositions of painters, like the *trompes l'oeil* of Samuel Hoogstraeten and the 'bird's-eye' views of parks and gardens by Jan

Siberechts. The *patte d'oie* or 'goose-foot' arrangement of avenues converging on the house, first introduced to England by the French gardener André Mollet, opened the way to a series of interconnecting spaces, all linked to the house – in the same way that hunting lodges like Ashdown in Berkshire had been placed at the centre of a star-shaped system of straight rides cut through the forest, affording spectators on the roof a view of the sport, and emphasizing the dominance of the house over the surrounding landscape.

Elizabethan hunting lodges, like Hardwick, were also among the first unfortified country houses to be built on hilltops. Less exposed situations were generally favoured throughout the seventeenth and early eighteenth centuries – Sir William Temple extolled the gently sloping site of Moor Park in Hertfordshire, and Timothy Nourse in his *Campania Foelix* (1700) recommended that a nobleman's seat should be erected 'not amongst Enclosures, but in a champaign, open Country'. Lord Tankerville's Uppark, built in the 1690s, high up on the Sussex Downs with distant views of the English Channel, is an exception to the rule, however, looking forward to the time when untamed nature would be admired rather than feared.

In Holland, where the small scale of estates rarely suited the limitless vistas of Le Nôtre, a much more static, compartmented garden, bounded by straight canals was the order of the day: the house itself occupying a central position only in the French-influenced palaces of William III and his immediate circle. Although Dutch influence can be strongly felt in the Gloucestershire gardens of Westbury and Dyrham, the Baroque parterres of William and Mary's English supporters likewise looked to France rather than the Low Countries for inspiration.

William Winde's great terraces at Cliveden in Buckinghamshire and Powis in North Wales are echoes of Saint-Germain, with martial overtones suitable for Lord Orkney, Britain's first Field-Marshal, and for the Herberts, who had inherited the greatest of the Welsh border fortresses. Vauban's forts were also the decisive influence on the gardens created by Sir John Vanbrugh in partnership with Charles Bridgeman at Blenheim, Grimsthorpe and Eastbury: their ramparts and bastions not only in keeping with the 'castle air' of Vanbrugh's houses, but also offering views into the neighbouring countryside, previously blocked by high boundary walls.

'The capital stroke, the leading step to all that has followed,' in Horace Walpole's words, was the introduction of another feature with a military origin: the sunk fence or 'ha-ha'. 'No sooner was this simple enchantment made,' he wrote in his *History of the Modern Taste in Gardening*, 'than levelling, mowing and rolling followed. The . . . park without the sunk fence was to be harmonised with the lawn within, and the garden in its turn was to be set free from its prim regularity, that it might assort with the wilder country without.' For Walpole, the undoubted hero of the hour was William Kent, who 'leaped the fence, and saw that all nature was a garden.' In fact Kent was by no means the first to use the ha-ha – Monsieur Beaumont, Colonel Graham's French gardener at Levens, had already made one there in the 1690s – and although Kent was undoubtedly the leading exponent of the early 'natural landscape' garden, there were many other economic, political and intellectual reasons for the revolution in taste which took Britain on such a different path to her Continental neighbours in the eighteenth century.

Under the Tudors, the dissolution of the monasteries and the enclosure system had already led to the creation of large landed estates, mostly supported by cattle- and sheep-grazing in place of the intensive arable farming that continued elsewhere in Europe. A new breed of resident landowners, who, unlike their counterparts in France and Germany, only rarely visited the capital and the court, also saw the commercial possibilities of woodlands, taking the advice of John Evelyn's *Sylva* (1664) and planting their demesnes with 'trees of venerable shade and profitable timber'. The many new species imported from the Mediterranean countries, from Scandinavia and America, also added to the colour and interest of the countryside beyond the garden walls.

A new style of gardening which was wholly compatible with existing agricultural practice, in Pope's words 'calling in the country', was bound to appeal to a class which identified so strongly with its lands. The economies to be made, compared with the upkeep of the formal garden, have perhaps been overstressed: Thomas Jefferson found fifteen men and eighteen boys at work at Stowe, and two hundred at Blenheim – fifty of them working on the Pleasure Grounds alone – while armies of men were needed for the levelling of hills and digging of lakes ordered by Capability Brown. But against this could be set the huge increases in the size of gardens, reflecting the ever-greater power of the Whig oligarchy.

The political and literary background of the 'Picturesque' movement was just as important as the economic. Rejecting the Baroque style of architecture as an expression of foreign absolutism, Lord Burlington and his followers proposed a return to the villas of classical antiquity, as described by Vitruvius, and interpreted by Palladio and

Inigo Jones. In very much the same way, they looked on the regimented lines of the Baroque garden (above all the perfect symmetry of Versailles) as a restriction of natural liberties, and urged a return to the landscapes described by the classical authors, notably Virgil, and interpreted by the painters Claude and Poussin. Balance was the quality they particularly sought – whether between hills and water, trees and bridges, temples and ruins, or even between square buildings and round ones – and this too had political connotations, for it was often held to express the balanced powers of the British constitution. The lack of variety in a formal layout, where the entire garden could be seen in one view from the main terrace, was also something to be avoided.

Instead of being the epicentre of the garden, the Palladian house gradually became no more than an incident within it. The idea of the circuit walk 'made through a succession of pictures', as Walpole put it, obviously started and ended with the house, and views back to it from different angles were composed with the greatest care to achieve a painterly effect. But smaller garden buildings, surprise views down on to lakes or rivers, cascades like Ruysdael's or hovels like Salvator Rosa's, could form equally satisfactory subjects. At Stourhead and at Studley Royal, two of the most famous 'Picturesque' landscapes, the house was actually situated outside the garden and could be seen from nowhere on the circuit walk. Elsewhere, its façades were treated as individual 'eyecatchers' to be spotted at different stages in the tour of the garden, like Nicholas Revett's portico at West Wycombe, always known as the 'Temple of Bacchus'. Richard Payne Knight even went so far as to remodel Downton Castle in Wiltshire so that it should look like the irregular, partly castellated farmhouses familiar from the landscapes of Claude, set high on its bluff above the river Wye, while in the 1830s the Husseys reduced their old castle at Scotney to a shell, and commissioned Salvin to build a new house on the hill above, with a terrace by William Sawrey Gilpin specially contrived to frame the newly picturesque ruin.

The total subservience of the house to its surroundings was stressed in two contrasting engravings in Payne Knight's *The Landscape*, published in 1794: the first showing a typical Georgian sash-windowed block set in a rather bleak parkland setting, with clumps of trees (which cattle have shorn of their lower branches) and a serpentine lake in the manner of Capability Brown; the second a much wilder scene of shaggy trees and boulders, with a rushing torrent, and the house beyond, remodelled as a 'Tudorbethan' pile, its skyline bristling with towers, obelisks and chimneystacks. Early in his career, Humphry Repton subscribed wholeheartedly to such principles –

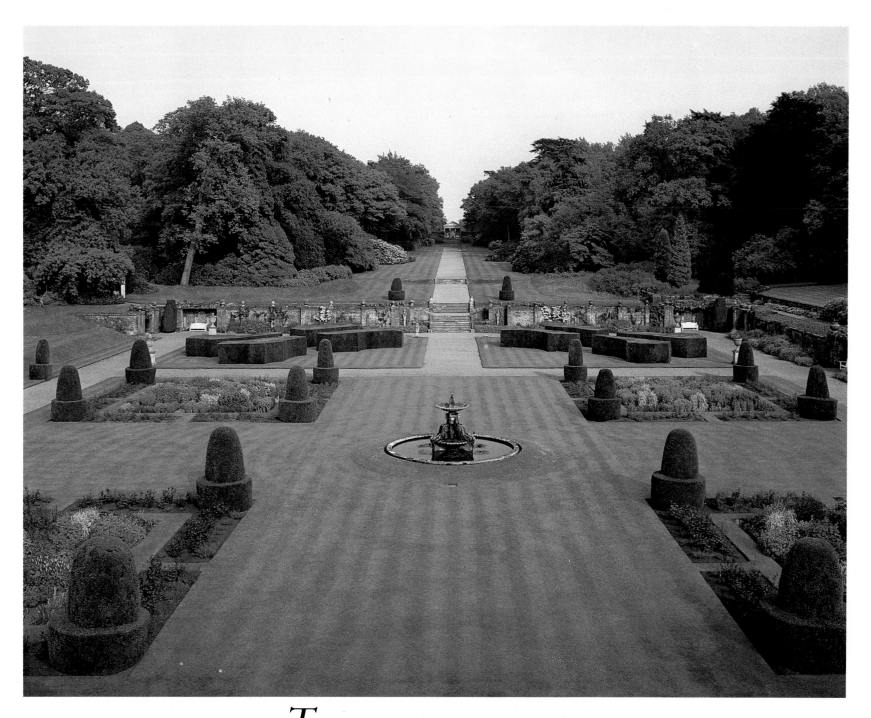

*T*hree centuries of growth: William Nesfield's parterre at
Blickling, laid out in 1872 and simplified by Norah Lindsay in the 1930s – with the early
eighteenth-century woodland garden and Doric Temple beyond.

The 'green parterre' on a huge scale, complementing the architecture of the country house: (above) a view from the roof of Cliveden in Buckinghamshire, with the river Thames in the background; (below) a view from the parapet at Chatsworth in Derbyshire, with the river Derwent beyond. To Garibaldi, who stayed at Cliveden in 1864, the very different vista of the Thames from Canning's oak (right) recalled 'some of the mightiest river prospects of South America'.

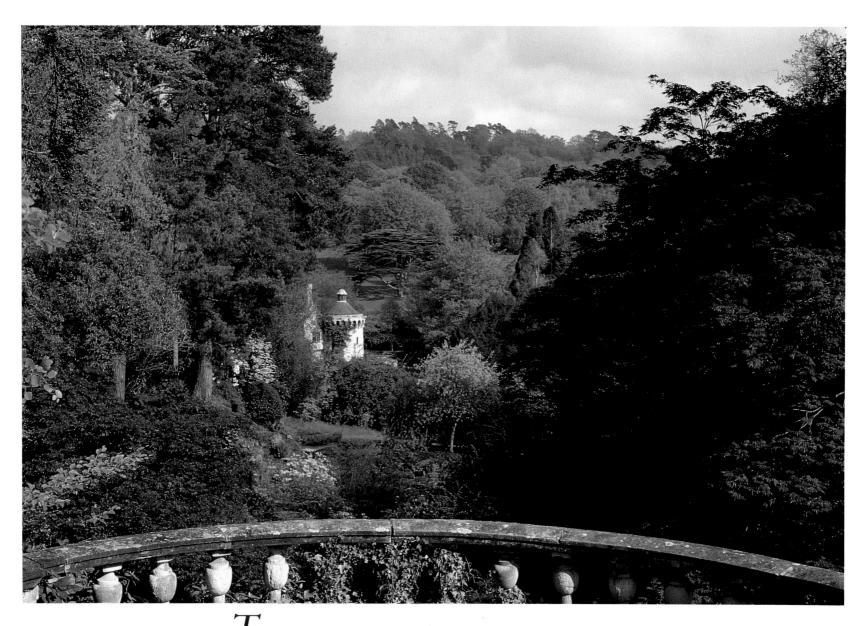

*T*he old castle at Scotney in Kent, seen from the terrace of Salvin's new house,
built in the 1830s: a quintessential statement of 'picturesque' principles, achieved with
the help of the landscape gardener, William Sawrey Gilpin.

for instance advising that towers of different heights be added to Blaise Castle in 1796. But by 1805 he was recommending a symmetrical arrangement of balustrade and flower-filled urns between the projecting wings of the garden front at Wimpole: in other words, bringing back formality to the immediate environs of the house.

The so-called 'gardenesque' style advocated by J. C. Loudon in the 1820s took this a stage further. Loudon had also begun as a thoroughgoing 'Picturesque' gardener following the principles of Payne Knight and Uvedale Price, but his extensive tours of the Continent between 1811 and 1821 and his conversion to the theories of Quatre-mère de Quincy, convinced him that gardens should be consciously differentiated from wild nature and recognizable as works of art. In his *Encyclopedia of Gardening* (1822) he also laid down the principle that each plant should be displayed to its best advantage. The vast numbers of new species and hybrids now being imported from every quarter of the globe, and cultivated in increasingly efficient hothouses, thus led to the eclecticism of Victorian garden design – the revival of formal parterres near the house, filled with bedding plants of brilliant hues and overlooked by Italianate terraces and steps; the rockeries for Alpine plants; the Japanese water gardens; the American shrubberies; the ferneries and pinetums – that still give gardens like Biddulph Grange and Alton Towers the feeling of horticultural museums, divided into type.

The 'Picturesque' style never entirely died – indeed in some respects it reached its apogee with houses like Cragside in Northumberland, perched above a ravine in a landscape, soon transformed from a lunar waste into a romantic fir-forest worthy of the brothers Grimm. But more often it was watered down to suit the tastes of plantsmen like William Robinson and his 'Surrey School', proud of the fact that their gardens grew out of the site and were never committed to plans on paper. This attitude was fiercely opposed by the architect Reginald Blomfield, following in the steps of Sir Charles Barry's great formal terraces at Trentham, Harewood and Shrubland, and in turn influencing Harold Peto's Buscot and Sir George Sitwell's Renishaw.

A synthesis between these opposite extremes was achieved by the partnership of an architect and a plantswoman, both of remarkable abilities: Edwin Lutyens and Gertrude Jekyll, who worked together on some seventy gardens between 1893 and 1912. Initially influenced by the Arts and Crafts movement and the cult of the cottage garden (which can be traced right back to the Regency period), Lutyens and Jekyll reintroduced a strong sense of unity between the vernacular house and its garden, successfully interlocking elements of their plan – a wing here, a pond there – by means of pergolas, loggias, steps and 'architectural' planting. 'Every garden scheme', Lutyens wrote, 'should have a backbone, a central idea beautifully phrased. Every wall, path, stone and flower should have its relationship to the central idea.' Lindisfarne off the Northumberland coast, Folly Farm in Berkshire and Hestercombe in Somerset are outstanding examples of their attention to detail, and use of local materials and traditions.

The two most famous gardens of the inter-war years, Laurence Johnston's Hidcote and V. Sackville-West's Sissinghurst, owe much to Gertrude Jekyll's restrained colour schemes, but also seem to evoke Dutch seventeenth-century designs in their strictly compartmented areas like 'outdoor rooms', each with a different character. Formal lines – tall yew hedges, pleached limes, walls, *clairvoyées* and rows of fruit trees – provide a foil for informal planting – herbaceous borders, ground cover, ornamental vegetables, clematis and rambling roses – to provide a mixture of grandeur and domesticity, rationalism and sentiment, in tune with the twentieth century's nostalgic view of the country house.

A setting for a Jacobean masque: the loggia at Cranborne Manor, Dorset.
(Right) A backdrop for a Victorian melodrama: the conifer woods at Cragside, Northumberland.

AVENUES, GATES AND GATEHOUSES

The approach to a country house, like the overture to an opera, needs to give the visitor an idea of what is to come: the scale of the estate, the rank of its owner, even perhaps the architectural style of the building. The unexpected can of course have its own excitement – a winding country lane with close-set hedgerows suddenly entering the park at Drayton, and disclosing the huge mass of the silvery-grey house like a village below, can catch the breath as much as the great lime avenues of its North-amptonshire neighbour, Boughton, planted along the skyline in the 1690s and still dwarfing the town of Kettering to the south.

Until at least the late seventeenth century, most country houses stood on or near a public road, and even though it was no

(Left) An eighteenth-century beech avenue at Drummond Castle, Perthshire
(Above) A sixteenth-century gatehouse at Charlecote in Warwickshire.

longer necessary to have a fully fortified gatehouse leading into a castle courtyard, as at Haddon or Hever, many Tudor and Elizabethan manors retained a gatehouse placed on axis with their newly centralized front doors, guarding a walled forecourt. That at Charlecote in Warwickshire built in 1550-51 has a large room over the central arch, which may have been used as a dormitory for household servants, though its smaller equivalent at Hardwick in Derbyshire has room only for a small porter's lodge, furnished with two beds, a table and two halberds in 1601. The gatehouse at Montacute in Somerset has disappeared, but it is interesting that both it and the flanking corner-pavilions of the courtyard (which still survive with their charming ogee roofs) are described as containing 'lodging chambers' in a survey of 1667.

The mason William Arnold, almost certainly the architect of Montacute, also designed the miniature gatehouse at Cranborne in Dorset, with its little pyramid-roofed pavilions set diagonally as if to invite the visitor to enter. The avenue that sweeps down to it is a comparatively recent replanting, but reflects standard late-seventeenth-century practice, when the boundaries of parks were beginning to be pushed back, particularly to make enclosures for deer. John Evelyn, in part of his unfinished *Elysium Britannicum* written in 1654, seems to have introduced the French word *avenue* to the English language, in the sense of being (as he put it) 'the principal walk to the front of the house'. It was also he who advocated limes as being the finest of all avenue trees, because of the regularity of their shape, and because even when planted close together their branches interweave without becoming stunted.

Ever since the Persian and Roman gardens of antiquity, avenues had been seen as symbols of authority, calling to mind rows of soldiers standing to attention, or forming a guard of honour. In the English countryside, with the gradual recession of the medieval forests, they took the place of the long straight rides that had approached the royal hunting lodges and their very length became a matter of pride. The double avenue of elms at Wimpole at Cambridgeshire, planted by Bridgeman in 1721 (and since replaced by limes) is three miles long and 500 feet wide, but even that was exceeded by the vast network of avenues laid out by the first Duke of Beaufort at Badminton in the 1690s.

At both Wimpole and Badminton the main avenues aligned on the entrance front were marginally wider than the façade they were to frame. Timothy Nourse in his *Campania Foelix* of 1700 appears to follow Le Nôtre's practice of tapering avenues so as to increase their apparent length, recommending that 'the Avenue or Approach may be cast into a Figure something resembling a Theatre; in which case we may allow what wideness we please, provided still that the principal Mansion, with all its Courts, Gardens, Out-buildings, and Offices, stand full in front to the Entrance, the shady Groves regularly contracting themselves the nearer Approach we make unto it.' He also subscribes to the current French fashion for an ironwork screen and gates to the forecourt, 'being of Azure and Gilded', instead of high walls and portals which would obscure the view of the house.

Jean Tijou's spectacular ironwork at Hampton Court for William and Mary was emulated by a whole generation of almost equally talented native blacksmiths, including Thomas Robinson in London, Robert Bakewell in Derbyshire and the Davies brothers in North Wales. Few of their forecourt screens survive in the position for which they were intended, but several of the finest were re-used as entrance gates to the park when the formal layout round the house was swept away in the mid-eighteenth century. Bakewell's magnificent screen at Cholmondeley in Cheshire seems always to have been painted white – like the Davies brothers' famous White Gates at Leeswood, near Mold – and early accounts more often refer to blue and green, with gilded ornaments, than to black. Heraldic ornaments – coats-of-arms and supporters – were also invariably picked out in the correct colours.

Before the introduction of the ha-ha, ironwork gates or grilles were also used as *clairvoyées* set into the high walls of the garden, often with avenues beyond them. Earlier in the seventeenth century, the idea had been to shut out the surrounding countryside altogether, and Inigo Jones' gateways at Oatlands in Surrey (followed by Nicholas Stone's in the Botanical Garden at Oxford) had been assertively classical, with solid timber doors, as if to stress the boundary between tamed and untamed nature. The Scottish architect Sir William Bruce had been one of the first to lead the eye beyond the garden wall with his gate on the main axis at Kinross, decorated with carved stone cornucopias and framing a view of the old house across the loch. The simple ironwork *clairvoyée* in the same position at Ham House dates from the 1670s, and may also have been designed by Bruce for his fellow-Scot, the Duke of Lauderdale. With the demise of the formal parterre under the influence of Kent and Bridgeman, only the kitchen garden was likely to retain its high walls, and this was usually entered through simpler, utilitarian doors – although at Castle Howard Vanbrugh's wonderfully flamboyant satyr gate seems to look back to the Italian Renaissance and the excesses of Bomarzo.

The approach to Castle Howard, still one of the most exciting experiences given to the country house visitor, was revolutionary in several ways. The site chosen by Vanbrugh and Lord Carlisle was intended to have spectacular views – rarely taken into consideration before this date – and the lake to the north prevented the usual straight avenue to the entrance front. Instead, Vanbrugh planned a huge new avenue rising and descending like a switchback, parallel with the main axis of the house, but about half a mile to the west. The Pyramid Gate, straddling this drive at one of its highest points, and flanked by battlemented walls, was consciously archaic in style, and a reference to the old castle of Henderskelfe, whose memory Lord Carlisle wished to perpetuate (both here and in the name of his new house) so as to stress the ancient lineage of his family.

Beyond the gate, the drive dipped sharply once again before climbing to a tall obelisk at the centre of a *rond-point*, where a right-angled turn led to the forecourt. Even from here the house was invisible, so another great obelisk was planned way beyond it in the middle of a pond in Wray Wood, beckoning the visitor on. Halfway there, the amazing length of Vanbrugh's palace would gradually have come into view and, making a second right-angled turn, the dazzled guest would mount the steps to the vast domed hall.

The idea of signposting changes of direction by obelisks, ultimately derived from Classical Rome, was a Baroque device which can for instance be found in Hawksmoor's plan for the rebuilding of Oxford. But used in the approach to a country house, it was a major innovation, as was the element of surprise. Though rejecting the straight lines and the formality of Castle Howard, the landscape gardeners of the following generation were to follow just this arrangement: a drive impelling the visitor from one 'picturesque' incident to another, eventually surprising him with a view of the house – the object of his journey – seen from the most flattering angle. At the same time Vanbrugh's gatehouse, while looking back to the Middle Ages, set the precedent for countless other eighteenth-century lodges and triumphal arches, placed so far from the house that they could afford to be substantial works of architecture in their own right.

The Pyramid Gate was used early on as a guesthouse for visiting gentry who came to see Castle Howard, and many later lodges were lived in by gamekeepers or other estate employees. Kent's Worcester Lodge at Badminton has a splendid dining room over the central arch, which is still used for shooting lunches; Sanderson Miller's

Gothick tower at Radway doubled up as a belvedere, from which he could show his guests the battlefield of Edgehill, while Kitty's Lodge at West Wycombe (called after a more than usually attractive gate-keeper) was built as a pair to Daphne's Temple, which had an open loggia on the far side acting as an eyecatcher from the gardens.

James Gibbs' symmetrical Boycott Pavilions of 1726, flanking the main drive at Stowe, were likewise intended for two quite different purposes: that on the garden side as an open pavilion with wide views to the south and east, that on the park side as a house for Lord Cobham's old friend and comrade-in-arms, Colonel Speed. As Gilbert West wrote in his poem on the gardens at Stowe, of 1732:

> On swelling Bastions here *Two* Buildings rise,
> Of *These*, a Shelter from the scorching Rays,
> One in the Garden Spreads its rustick Base:
> One in the Park, an habitable Frame,
> The Household *Lares*, and *Penates* claim.

Only a few lodges were actually conceived as eyecatchers from a house, and of these the noblest must be the Corinthian Arch at Stowe. This was built in 1767 at the point where the long avenue from Buckingham climbs to the edge of the park, and a great panorama of the house, park and lake unfolds. Its giant scale and windowless simplicity also make it a striking silhouette on the skyline seen from the south front, although the architect Thomas Pitt, Lord Camelford, ingeniously provided two sizeable houses for groundsmen or keepers within – their windows arranged in three storeys on the east and west elevations.

The triumphal arch, a favourite theme of neo-classical architects, was particularly appropriate for a lodge which terminated a village street, like Hawksmoor's arch at Blenheim and Chambers' at Wilton, or Lewis Wyatt's entrance to Tatton Park from the little Cheshire town of Knutsford. Robert Adam varied the theme at Syon Park in Middlesex by adding open colonnades each side of the central arch, which provided pedestrian entrances, but also acted as a kind of *clairvoyée* into the landscaped park – much less forbidding than the usual high stone walls. The elaborate decorative detail, preparing the visitor for Adam's sumptuous state rooms inside the house, was carried out in Coade stone, a kind of terracotta which could be moulded and fired. Its remarkable durability made it a favourite material for the ornament of lodges and garden buildings in the eighteenth century, until the secret of its manufacture was lost.

'The park-gate of Sion-house is certainly elegant,' wrote W. S. Gilpin, in his

Remarks on Forest Scenes of 1791, 'but it raises the idea of a stile of architecture, which you must drop, when you arrive at the house.' As one of the most advanced theorists of the 'Picturesque', Gilpin was against follies and eyecatchers in general, although 'one ornament of this kind, I should be inclined to allow, and that is a handsome gate at the entrance of the park . . . which should be proportioned in richness, and elegance to the house, and should also correspond with it in stile.' The range of historical styles employed in the early nineteenth century, from Thomas Hopper's neo-Norman gatehouse at Penrhyn to William Legg's neo-Tudor 'Bottle Lodges' at Burghley, shows that many of his contemporaries shared this view – while Sir John Soane's remarkable entrance arch at Tyringham, stripped of all classical detail and looking forward almost to the architecture of the Bauhaus, shows how innovative and experimental such buildings could afford to be, compared with the country houses they served.

Although the winding serpentine drive had almost entirely replaced the straight avenue by the 1740s, it was not long before a reaction set in. 'The reformation seems to me to have been pushed too far,' wrote Horace Walpole in 1771, '. . . a great avenue cut through woods, perhaps before entering a park, has a noble air, and

> "Like footmen running before coaches
> To tell the inn what Lord approaches"

announces the habitation of some man of distinction.' Repton's 'Red Books' often recommend that part of the drive should make use of an old avenue, even if the rest was enlivened with views of bridges, water, woods and the other 'artificial obstructions', which (in Gilpin's words) 'Mr Brown was often very happy in creating'.

In the nineteenth century a renewed passion for evergreen trees and shrubs and the availability of new species encouraged the idea of woodland drives underplanted with rhododendrons and many a Victorian house now lies at the end of an almost impenetrable tunnel of *ponticum*. Prince Albert's avenues at Osborne in the Isle of Wight, lined with mixed trees, many of tropical origin, also gave birth to some strange progeny, like the avenue of alternate Wellingtonias and monkey-puzzles at Erddig – looking oddly exotic in rural North Wales. Yet if the approaches to the country house can be eccentric, that too is an accurate foretaste of what is to come: a lovable mixture of different styles and tastes in gardening, whether historical or historicist, formed by many generations of the same family – a link with the past that is every bit as fascinating as the rooms in which they lived.

Echoes of Imperial Rome: William Kent's obelisk at Holkham, built in 1729, with the monument to Coke of Norfolk seen beyond.

A lime avenue at Nymans in Sussex (above) and (right) the walled
forecourt at Cranborne Manor, Dorset, with its lozenge-shaped lodges built in 1620,
probably to the designs of the master-mason William Arnold.

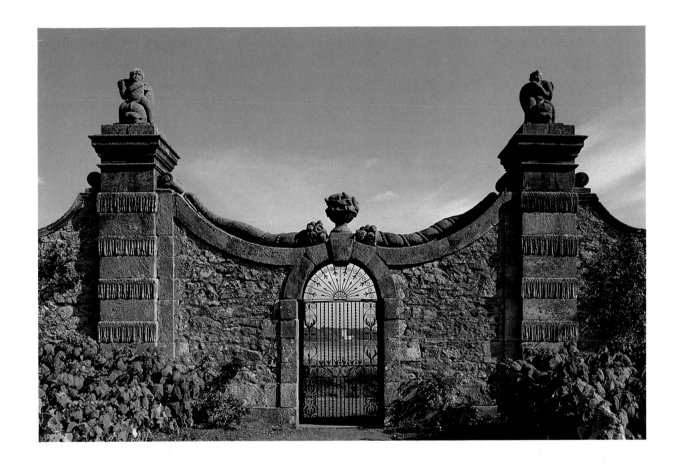

*T*asselled spears in wrought-iron form a palisade, guarding the forecourt at Blenheim Palace (left)
(Above) Sir William Bruce's 'clairvoyée' at Kinross, known as the Fish Gate from the carved stone basket in
the centre, containing the seven varieties of fish to be found in Loch Leven. Placed on the
main axis of his new house, completed in 1693, the gate also frames a view of the old castle of the
Douglases of Morton, seen across the blue waters of the loch.

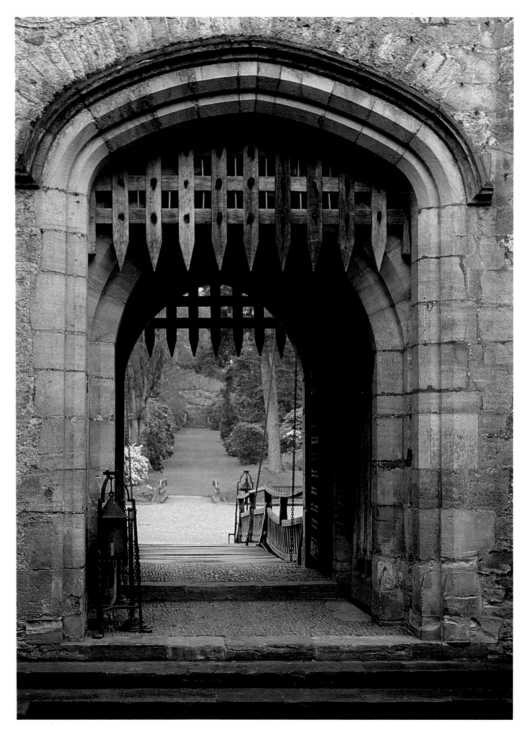

The forbidding approach to a medieval house: portcullises and a drawbridge at Hever Castle in Kent. The gatehouse here was built by Sir John de Cobham soon after 1384.

The eighteenth-century gate screen, designed to attract friends rather than repel enemies. This example at Cholmondeley Castle in Cheshire, attributed to the Davies brothers of Wrexham, came from the forecourt of the old house, remodelled by Vanbrugh.

Guardians of the gate: (above) an early seventeenth-century copy of a famous antique – the bronze statue of Marcus Aurelius outside the Capitol in Rome – placed on Sir William Chambers' triumphal arch at Wilton in 1755; (below left) the Percy lion on Adam's gate screen at Syon Park; and (below right) the Yorke stag on the Arrington gates at Wimpole. (Right) Seventeenth-century brick piers, and eighteenth-century ironwork, at Packwood in Warwickshire.

PARTERRES AND KNOT GARDENS

Nothing illustrates the fickleness of fashion in gardening so well as the parterre. Having been the lynchpin of the layout throughout the Tudor and Stuart periods, it was virtually banished from the Georgian country house until rediscovered by Repton in the early nineteenth century. After full rehabilitation in the vast formal gardens of W. A. Nesfield, it descended to the level of municipal park planting towards the end of the Victorian period, and is only now being re-adopted by those who view the lost gardens of the sixteenth and seventeenth centuries with nostalgia – and who are bored with the amoeba-shaped beds of the 'Surrey School'.

Once again, the essential quadripartite shape of the parterre is

The restored knot garden in front of the old Bishop's Palace at Hatfield (above), and the east parterre (right) – planted by John Tradescant in 1607-12.

of immense antiquity. According to the Book of Genesis, 'a river went out of Eden to water the garden and from thence it was parted, and became four heads.' The *chahar bagh* or 'fourfold garden' of Islamic culture goes back to at least 6000 bc, evidently deriving from the same basic tradition, and it was from Persia, through the Byzantines, that the form was first introduced to Europe – together with the idea of raised banks or seats of turf, and surrounding borders of flowers. These enclosed gardens, often with four paths leading to a fountain at the centre, usually lay immediately below the windows of first-floor solars or chambers, and hence the need for a pleasing geometrical shape seen from above, which was to become one of the chief characteristics of the parterre. Interestingly, the cloister seems not to have contributed to its development (early monastic accounts speaking only of turf and the occasional tree), although the idea of tunnel-like arbours round the four sides of the parterre – derived above all from Burgundy – may be a reminiscence of its covered walks.

Early on, the different sections of the parterre were likely to be treated either as plain lawn or with different flowers sown broadcast in clover – the so-called 'flowery meads' familiar from French *millefleur* tapestries of the fifteenth century. The idea of patterns of 'knots' of interlacing bands (based on the symbol for infinity: ∞) caught on early in the sixteenth century, however, many of them influenced by Francesco Colonna's *Hypnerotomachia Poliphili*, published in Venice in 1499, with diagrams which the author related to *tapeti* or carpets. In a rare description of Henry VIII's privy garden at Hampton Court, the German Thomas Platter, exactly a hundred years later, noticed 'numerous patches where square cavities had been scooped out, as for paving stones; some of these were filled with red brick-dust, some with white sand, and some with green lawn, very much resembling a chess-board.' Similar knots at Richmond Palace in 1501 were made in the form of 'marvellous beasts, as lions, dragons, and such other of divers kinds, properly fashioned and carved in the ground, right well sanded, and compassed with lead.'

Gervase Markham, in *The English Husbandman* of 1613, differentiates between these 'open knots', where the pattern was set out in lines of rosemary, thyme or some other herb and the intervening spaces filled with coloured earth or sand, and 'closed knots' where the spaces were filled with flowers. The former seem already to have been going out of fashion by 1625, however, when Francis Bacon remarked that 'as for the making of knots or figures, with divers coloured earths that they may lie under the windows of the house on that side which the garden stands, they be but toys; you may variegated evergreens, rose hedges and flowering shrubs to achieve a wholly different effect – very much a romantic's view of the old Scottish garden. In the same way, W. A. Nesfield, a successful painter before he took to garden design, often based his formal parterres on old pattern-books, like d'Argenville's *La Theorie et la practique du jardinage* (1709), but made them far bolder and more architectural in effect with Irish yews, terracotta balustrades and fountain basins.

The huge greenhouses of the time, and the armies of gardeners available, vastly increased the scale of 'bedding-out' – the system whereby parterre beds would be filled with different flowering plants for different times of the year. The pioneers of bedding in the 1830s were George Fleming at Trentham Park in Staffordshire and Donald Beaton at Shrubland Park in Suffolk, while the addition of spring bulbs to the repertoire was first introduced by John Fleming at Cliveden. Significantly, all three were great Italianate houses designed by Sir Charles Barry, and Barry's skill in providing the architectural framework for their horticultural experiments was of crucial importance for the development of the Victorian garden.

In the twentieth century, many of the great formal parterres were simplifed not only for economic reasons, but because the strident colours of pelargoniums, petunias, salvias and lobelias were going out of fashion. In their place, followers of Gertrude Jekyll like Norah Lindsay (who modified Nesfield's parterre at Blickling) substituted the perennials of the herbaceous border, carefully graded in size to achieve pyramid effects in each bed. At the same time carpet-bedding, using dwarf or creeping foliage plants in contrasting patterns, became increasingly the preserve of the municipal park, and was replaced by less complicated blocks of softer colour, using plants like santolina and senecio – as at Cliveden. New parterres are still being laid out, ranging from the west garden at Chatsworth, with the ground-plan of Lord Burlington's villa at Chiswick simply executed in cut box, to that at Holker in Cumbria, where ornamental cabbages and standard honeysuckles vie with more conventional annuals and perennials in the border. Here among busts and urns, garden seats and trellis obelisks – all symmetrically arranged round the smoothest of croquet lawns – they represent an eclectic, 1980s response to the old challenge of the formal parterre.

Sir William Bruce's gardens at Kinross in Fifeshire were planted and had become famous even before the great Scottish architect embarked on the rebuilding of the house. Sir Charles Lyttleton, writing from London in 1688, had heard that 'Lady Lauderdale's gardens at Ham are but a wilderness compared to yours'. Some of the main French-inspired features still survive, including the axial path aligned on an old island castle in Loch Leven.

A romantic's view of the old Scottish garden:
the great parterre at Drummond Castle, Perthshire, recreated in the 1820s
and 1830s by George and Lewis Kennedy.
*(Above) The view from the upper terrace, showing the overall plan in
the form of St Andrew's Cross. (Below) The fountain garden to the south-east.
(Left) The 'Crown', with flowering shrubs and variegated evergreens,
within box-edged beds.*

*P*eacocks on a balustrade at Dyrham Park in Gloucestershire. Perched on walls, or spreading
their tails on great flights of steps, they have always been perfect foils to the formality of the parterre.
(Right) Lady Salisbury's new knot garden at Cranborne Manor, Dorset, seen from an upstairs
window – a modern design perfectly in harmony with the seventeenth-century house.

55

TOPIARY AND MAZES

The art of topiary, shaping trees and shrubs by clipping them, expresses man's need to tame the wildness of nature at its most basic. The word derives ultimately from the Greek *topia* meaning landscapes, through the Latin *opus topiarium*, used to describe the whole art of ornamental gardening rather than in the narrower modern sense. However, Pliny the Elder refers in his *Naturalis Historia* to cypress trees being cut into tableaux – 'hunt-scenes, fleets of ships, and all sorts of images' – and ascribes the invention of tree-clipping to a Roman named G. Matius, active at the end of the first century bc. The younger Pliny's account of the garden at his Tuscan villa also mentions 'box, which is cut into a thousand shapes or even letters, which sometimes spell out the name of the owner, sometimes that of the designer.'

Topiary at Levens Hall, Cumbria (above and right) originally planted by the French gardener Guillaume Beaumont between 1689 and 1712.

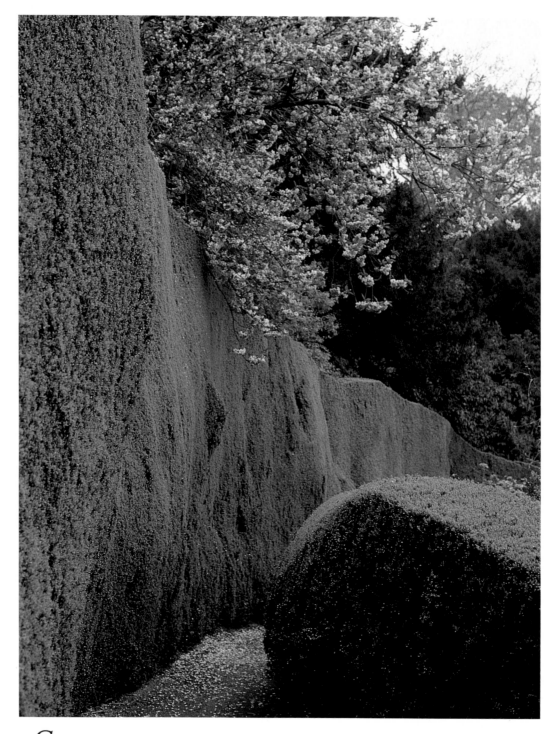

*S*olid walls of yew, overhung with cherry blossom, on the terraces at Powis Castle, North Wales.

*T*opiary as architecture: (above) the yew arbour at Drummond Castle, (below) the buttresses below the terrace at Pitmedden.

*T*he *maze at Hever Castle (left), in the angle of the medieval moat, with the monogram of its creator, William Waldorf Astor, planted in box at the entrance. (Above) A yew hedge with 'windows' at Cranborne Manor, of a type known in France in the early eighteenth century as a 'Palissade de Chantilly'. John James, who illustrated similar hedges in his* Theory and Practice of Gardening *(1712), urged their use for 'Galleries, Porticoes, Halls and Green Vistas'.*

*C*ottage-garden topiary in the White Garden at Hidcote (above) – praised by V. Sackville-West as being 'in the country tradition of smug broody hens, bumpy doves and coy peacocks' – contrasted with the simpler geometry of the 'brackets' round a square pool at Crathes Castle, Kincardineshire (left) planted in 1932, and (right) the stepped planes of yew surrounding the lily pond at Knightshayes in Devon.

FLOWER GARDENS AND BORDERS

Flowers have exercised a fascination for man from the beginning of time, despite the fact that they are of less practical use to him than almost any other natural phenomena. The fact that so many of their names originate in Greek myth – narcissus, hyacinth, daphne, not to mention the nymph Flora, herself supposed to have given the world the seeds of countless varieties – shows how potent their symbolism was, even in antiquity. In the monastic gardens of the Middle Ages, flowers were likewise seen as emblems of Christian virtues: above all the lily, whose white colour and sweet smell were associated with the purity and sanctity of the Virgin Mary; and the rose, signifying the blood of Our Saviour, just as its prickles suggested the crown of thorns. The

(Left) The rose garden at Syon Park in Middlesex. Begun in 1967, it now covers ten acres, and contains over two hundred different varieties.

Benedictines were particularly devoted to the cultivation of flowers, illustrating them as borders to their missals, and giving them characteristics such as those listed by the Catholic Henry Hawkins in his *Partheneia Sacra* of 1633: 'the *Violet* of Humilitie, the Gilloflower of Patience, the Marygold of Charitie, the *Hiacinth* of Hope, the *Sun-flower* of Contemplation.'

Cut flowers were used in interiors from an early date, particularly to obviate the smells that were rife before the invention of the water-closet, and the nosegays still carried in the Lord Mayor of London's processions are a reminder of how necessary they were outdoors as well as indoors. Many medieval flower gardens, like the one belonging to the nuns of Romsey, recorded as being accessible to outsiders as early as 1092, may thus have been run on commercial lines. The thin flower borders used to edge grass plots in the walled 'pleasure garden' were usually composed of specimen flowering plants, probably with more thought for their exoticism than for their appearance *en masse*. The 'closed knots' of clipped hedges filled with flowers of one colour carried this a stage further, but perhaps the first evidence of flowers being grouped in a painterly way comes in Sir Henry Wotton's *Elements of Architecture* (1624), describing 'the Garden of Sir *Henry Fanshaw*, at his seat in *Ware-Parke*, where I wel remember, hee did so precisely examine the *tinctures*, and *seasons* of his *flowres*, that in their *setting*, the *inwardest* of those which were to come up at the same time, should be alwayes a little *darker* than the *outmost*, and to serve them for a kinde of gentle *shadow*, like a piece not of *Nature*, but of *Arte*.'

Scents were also considered of the greatest importance in the sixteenth and seventeenth centuries, and again they could have symbolic connotations, as we are reminded by the romantic inscription on a marquetry table-top in the High Great Chamber at Hardwick – 'The redolent smelle of eglantyne/we stagges extol to the divyne' (a reference to the stags supporting the Cavendish coat-of-arms). Francis Bacon gives whole lists of flowers whose '*Breath* . . . is farre Sweeter in the Aire . . . then in the hand,' and which were evidently intended to be planted together, in beds or borders near the house, particularly recommending 'Wall-Flowers, which are very Delightfull, to be set under a Parler, or lower Chamber window'. Honeysuckles he seems to have thought too strong, however, unless 'they be somewhat a farre off '.

The increasing interest in the natural world that characterized early-seventeenth-century thought, leading to the discoveries of Newton and the founding of the Royal

*T*he Lupin Garden at Chatsworth, planted recently on part of the site of Paxton's Great Conservatory.
(Right) The celebrated White Garden at Sissinghurst, created by V. Sackville-West in the 1930s, and inspired
by some of Gertrude Jekyll's earlier theories on the use of colour.

A yellow border at Great Dixter in Sussex (above), complementing the rose-red brick and tiled roofs of old barns and oast-houses. (Below) A bold planting of tulips and forget-me-nots at Nymans, in the same county. (Left) Yellow and red flowers grouped in the sunken garden at Packwood House, Warwickshire, created in the 1930s by Graham Baron Ash.

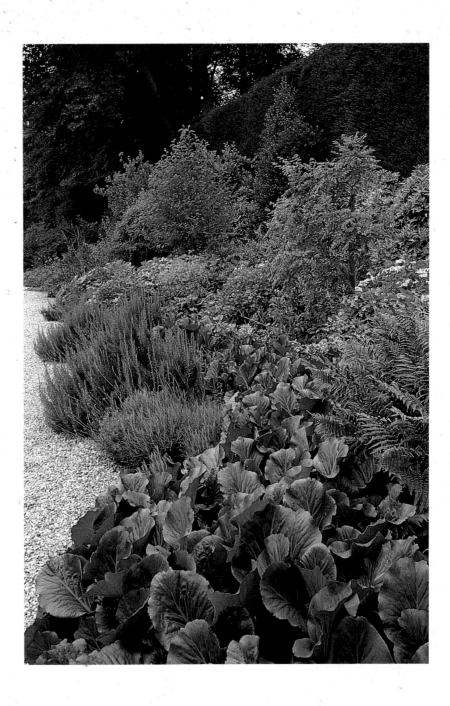

*W*ide herbaceous borders flanking a narrow path at Crathes Castle, Kincardineshire (left). Gardens
like these fulfil Gertrude Jekyll's dictum that earth should never be visible in a flower-bed – except in winter.
(Above) A border at Dyrham Park in Gloucestershire showing a mixture of herbs and herbaceous plants, with
a controlled colour scheme of silver-grey foliage and soft pink flowers.

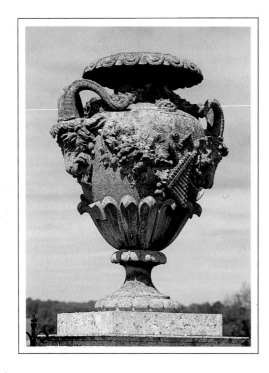

STATUES, URNS AND VASES

The humanism of the Italian Renaissance – the setting of man at the centre of an ordered universe – received one of its clearest expressions in the idea of the sculpture garden, where nature was not only tamed but also dominated by representations of the human form. Bramante's Belvedere Court at the Vatican, begun about 1505 for Pope Julius II, was perhaps the first to revive the idea, its use of excavated Greek and Roman statues emphasizing the link with the gardens of classical antiquity, and illustrating the Arcadian visions of Virgil, or the empathy between living forms found in Ovid's *Metamorphoses*. Gardens of the early English Renaissance were more likely to be furnished with heraldic imagery, like the painted wooden statues of the King's Beasts

One of a pair of stone vases carved with pan-pipes and goat's masks at Wimpole, Cambridgeshire. (Right) Lead putti and vases alternate on the terrace at Wilton House, near Salisbury.

at Henry VIII's Hampton Court. But a number of columns and obelisks from the garden at Nonsuch are illustrated in the famous Lumley Inventory of 1590, and their brightly coloured marbles suggest that some at least may have been brought back from Lord Lumley's embassy to Florence in the 1570s.

The first true sculpture garden in England was the creation of Lord Lumley's great-nephew, the Earl of Arundel, who took Inigo Jones to Italy, and who acquired there the first important collection of classical antiquities to reach these shores. While some of the finest statues were displayed in a sculpture gallery overlooking the Thames at Arundel House, others were arranged on plinths and balustrades in the raised parterre between the house and the Strand – as depicted in the background of the Earl's portrait, now at Welbeck. Francis Bacon, who felt that '*Statua's*, and such Things' added 'State, and Magnificence, but nothing to the true Pleasure of a Garden', was presumably being sarcastic when he visited Arundel House and 'coming into the . . . Garden, where there were a great number of Ancient Statues of naked Men and Women, made a stand, and as astonish'd cryed out: *The Resurrection*.' On the other hand, Charles I was so struck by the idea that he sent Hubert le Sueur to Rome to take moulds of the most famous classical sculptures for the gardens at St James's, while Nicholas Stone's rather lumpish statues of Venus and Cupid, Diana and other deities, which still survive at Wilton, show how native sculptors were quick to take up the theme.

Just as the Elizabethan and Stuart parterre was often conceived as the setting for court masques, so its statues could be seen as actors, enhancing the associational value of the garden. Perhaps the best example of this is Sir John Danvers' garden at Chelsea, begun in 1622, whose scheme has been interpreted by Roy Strong as an evocation of Arcadia, very much in tune with Samuel Daniel's masques for Anne of Denmark, the *Queens Arcadia* (1605) and *Hymen's Triumph* (1614). The sphinxes guarding the main entrance to the garden symbolized the search for ancient wisdom, while the flanking statues of Cain and Abel, and Hercules and Antaeus, represented the search for lost innocence before man's fall, and the defeat of earthly passions – the one biblical, the other classical. Then in the garden itself Aubrey described statues (again by Nicholas Stone) depicting 'the Faithful Shepherd, and the Faithfull Shepherdesse . . . expressing Love-passions in the very freestone: where you read rustick beauty mixt with antique innocent simplicitie.' Again the inspiration for such complex imagery probably came from Italy, and it is interesting to find John Evelyn visiting the Palazzo Negrone at Genoa in 1644 and finding 'a grove of stately trees, furnish'd with artificial

Sheepe, Shepheards, & Wild Beasts, so naturaly cut in a grey-stone . . . [that] you would imagine yourselfe in a Wildernesse & Silent Country, side-ways in the heart of a great Citty.'

Evelyn's travel diaries of the 1640s show his particular excitement at the amount of statuary in French and Italian gardens, drawing lessons for its display in the harsher English climate. Thus the 'incomparable statues' in the Belvedere Court 'are for defence against the Weather shut up in their Neeches with dores of Wainscot', while at the Villa Medici on the Pincian Hill, 'here is also a row balustr'd with white marble, on which are erected divers statues and heads, covered over with the natural shrubbs, Ivys & other perennial Greenes, as in nices.' The disintegration of stone and marble outdoors was a perennial problem, however, and it was partly for this reason that lead-work became so popular in the late seventeenth century. The whole point of statues, according to John Woolridge writing in 1677, was for 'Winter diversion . . . to re-compence the loss of past pleasures, and to buoy up hope of another Spring,' so the boxing-in practised in colder countries like Russia from an early date was rarely fol-lowed in England.

Large numbers of lead figures by Jan Van Nost and his successor, Andries Carpen-tière, survive in English country-house gardens, but their weathered and lichened appearance which we have come to admire is very different from the sculptors' orig-inal intention. Seventeenth- and eighteenth-century accounts invariably record their being painted to resemble stone or marble, brass or bronze, or even in polychrome. A visitor to John Cheere's famous statuary yard at Hyde Park Corner in the 1750s described the figures 'cast in lead as large as life and frequently painted with an inten-tion to resemble nature. They consisted of Punch, Harlequin, Columbine and other pantomimical figures; mowers whetting their scythes, haymakers resting on their rakes, gamekeepers in the act of shooting and Roman soldiers with firelocks, but above all that of an African, kneeling with a sundial on his head.' The lead slave trade was evidently brisk, for a number of examples of the blackamoor sundial still exists, many of them bearing traces of red, green and yellow paint on their feathered skirts and head-dresses.

The sundial had been thought an appropriate ornament for the garden since at least the beginning of the sixteenth century, Brise Augustyn of Westminster supply-ing no less than twenty for Hampton Court in June 1534. The demonstration of sci-ence, as in the automata of Salomon de Caus's grottoes, or the orrery on a column recommended by John Woolridge, was one aspect of its popularity, but its emblematic value was still more powerful. The garden, with its cycle of seasons, was a constant reminder of the transitory nature of man's existence:

> As Time and Howres paseth awaye
> So doeth the life of man decaye
> As Time can be redeemed with no cost
> Bestow it well and let no houre be lost.

Pillars too were looked on as symbolic and appropriate ornaments, representing justice and strength of purpose. The large column in the centre of the Great Garden at Wimbledon was erected in the 1590s, probably in conscious tribute to the crowned pillar device of Elizabeth I, while another in porphyry seen at Wilton by Daniel Defoe, and 32 feet high, was used to support a marble statue of Venus.

Very precise instructions as to the placing of the different deities can be found in eighteenth-century treatises on gardening. As Stephen Switzer put it, in his *Ichnographia Rustica* in 1718, 'it cann't but be an unpleasant Sight . . . to view *Jupiter*, *Mars*, *Neptune*, and the rest of the capital Deities of Heaven, misplac'd, and by a meanness of spirit below a good Designer, set perching upon a little Pedestal; one like a Citizen; a second with a Pike in his Hand, like a Foot-Soldier; and the third upon dry Land with a Trident, like a Cart-filler.' Batty Langley's *New Principles of Gardening*, published ten years later, gives detailed lists of the figures suitable for different locations, descending to some of the lower slopes of Olympus for inspiration: thus Flora and Cloris might be attended in the flower garden by '*Runcina* the Goddess of Weeding'; Diana and Actaeon could be accompanied in 'Woods and Groves' by Philomela who was transformed into a nightingale, and Itis who became a pheasant; while 'small Inclosures of Wheat, Barley, &c. in a Wilderness' might suit '*Robigus* a God who preserved Corn from being blasted . . . and *Tutelina* a Goddess, who had the Tuition of Corn in the Fields.'

Garden statues could also convey a political message. At Stowe, Rysbrack's series of the Saxon gods and goddesses who gave their name to the days of the week recalled the 'ancient liberties' of druidical Britain, in the same way as his busts for the Temple of British Worthies, including King Alfred and the Black Prince, gave an illustrious pedigree to Lord Cobham's brand of patriotic Whiggery. As the taste for 'Picturesque' gardening grew, however, statues began to be thought too artificial as ornaments for a purely landscape setting, and urns or vases were preferred. In William Shenstone's words, 'Urns are more solemn, if large and plain; more beautiful, if less and orna-mented. Solemnity is perhaps their print, and the situation of them should still coop-erate with it.' Orange and bay trees placed outdoors in the summer had in the seventeenth century been placed in gilded lead or blue-and-white China or Delft vases, as can be seen in the famous Stoke Edith needlework hangings – or in painted Versailles tubs, which would take larger specimens, as in Peter Rysbrack's painting of the Orange Tree Garden at Chiswick. But these too were considered gaudy, and out of key with the muted colours of nature, by Capability Brown's day.

Chaste neo-classical urns made of Coade stone and based on celebrated antique prototypes, like the Warwick Vase, were thought more suitable incidents on the ser-pentine walks of *fermes ornées* like Shenstone's own at the Leasowes. Latin inscriptions and dedications invoked the world of Homer and Virgil, and urns were dedicated to the memory of friends to provide a tinge of pleasing melancholy. At Shugborough, the Shepherds Monument consisted of a bas-relief by Scheemakers after Poussin's famous *Et in Arcadia Ego*, one of the most potent images of the 'Picturesque' movement, breathing the same air of mystery that haunts Keats' 'Ode to a Grecian Urn'.

Repton's restoration of the terrace as a podium for the house in the early years of the nineteenth century also restored the fashion for statues and vases – filled with trailing plants in the Italian manner – lining stone or terracotta balustrades. Matthew Digby Wyatt's new formal gardens at Castle Ashby, dating from the 1840s, were bounded by balustrades inspired by the Jacobean lettering round the parapet of the house – but instead of the psalms in Latin, somewhat gloomy quotations in English from the Song of Solomon (including 'The grass withereth and fadeth away . . .') were rendered in four-foot-high terracotta letters. A revival of interest in the gardens of the Italian Renaissance persuaded William Waldorf Astor at the end of the century to acquire the famous balustrade from the forecourt of the Villa Borghese in Rome, though the authorities prevented him from acquiring the antique statues that stood on it. When the balustrade was re-erected below the terrace at Cliveden in the 1890s, it was thus crowned with a pair of handmaidens of Diana, carved by Poirier and Cayot for Louis XIV's Marly – not perhaps correct from a purist point of view but splendid in scale and in their picturesque effect. Both at Cliveden and at Hever Castle, which he acquired in 1906, Astor's Roman sarcophagi placed against dark yew hedges, stone urns silhouetted against the sky, and use of statues to emphasize the perspective of a long vista, can be compared with the work of Harold Peto at Buscot or Achille

Duchêne at Blenheim; a mixture of formality with romantic yearning that can also be found at the turn of the century in illustrated books on French and Italian gardens.

One of the most remarkable collections of English garden sculpture is that at Anglesey Abbey, in the garden which the first Lord Fairhaven began to lay out in 1926, on an unpromising stretch of flat Cambridgeshire fen. Rysbrack's *Father Time* supporting a sundial in the centre of the Herbaceous Garden, the ten Corinthian columns from Chesterfield House set round the circular Temple Lawn, or the six Coade stone caryatids from Soane's Bank of England marking the cross-axis in the Great Avenue to a large extent dictate the form of their new settings, and can be compared with the antique furniture collected for neo-Georgian interiors in the 1930s. Since the War a few notable attempts have been made to create gardens round contemporary sculpture – as at Sutton Place, where the Ben Nicholson 'wall', a huge white marble relief, is mirrored in a formal lily pond designed by Sir Geoffrey Jellicoe. But far the most successful synthesis between art and nature has been achieved at Glenkiln in Dumfriesshire, where Henry Moore's King and Queen (among other sculptures) gaze majestically over a Scottish grouse moor – not perhaps a garden in the accepted sense, but a return to the 'Picturesque', and to Burke's ideals of the Beautiful and the Sublime.

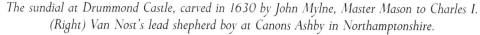

The sundial at Drummond Castle, carved in 1630 by John Mylne, Master Mason to Charles I. (Right) Van Nost's lead shepherd boy at Canons Ashby in Northamptonshire.

A garden bestiary: (above) the Wild Boar at Castle Howard, a lead copy of the famous antique statue in the Uffizi, plays host to visiting peacocks; (below left) a monkey, supporting Van Nost's giant Vase of the Seasons at Melbourne in Derbyshire; and (below right) a sacred cow, in the Chinese garden at Biddulph Grange, Staffordshire. (Left) one of a pair of kneeling slaves at Melbourne, also by Van Nost, supplied in 1700 at a cost of £30.

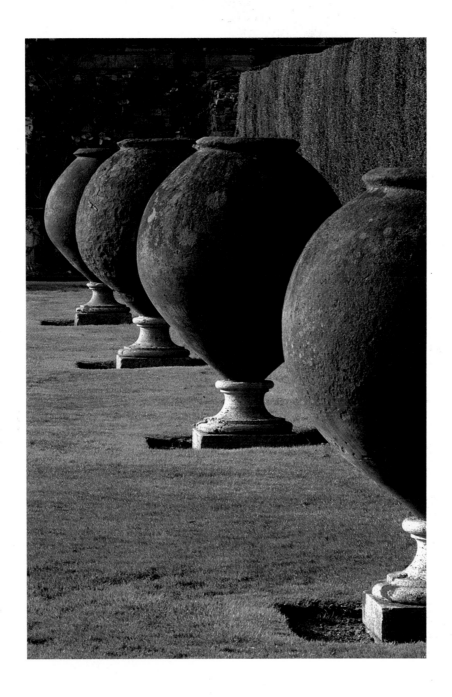

*E*dwardian opulence: antique terracotta jars at Hever Castle, brought back from the Middle East
by William Waldorf Astor, and (left) Italian copies of Greek and Roman statues in the 9th Duke of Marlborough's
Water Garden at Blenheim Palace. The sphinx is said to have been modelled with the features (and
the long neck) of his wife, the American heiress, Consuelo Vanderbilt.

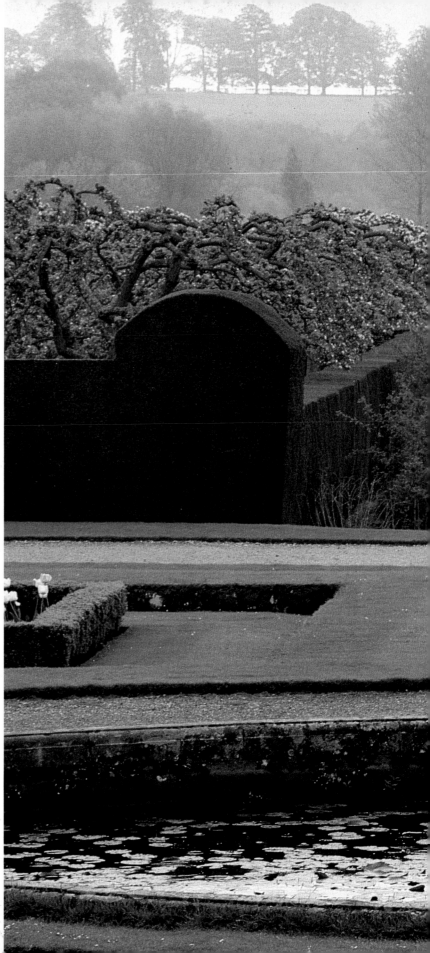

*S*culpture as a focal point: (above) one of a number of
sundials telling the passing of the hours in the garden at Penshurst in Kent;
(below) the Byzantine urn in the Sunk Garden at Nymans; and
(right) a copy of the Belvedere Antinous in the centre of the parterre at
Penshurst – a souvenir of Italy among the orchards of the Weald.

ALLEES AND VISTAS

The difference between the *allée* and the avenue (both words of French derivation) is one of scale, but also implies a different use: the former, a walk within the garden proper; the latter, a drive in the park beyond. In the French formal garden, the *allées*, bordered by pollarded trees, clipped hedges or simply lawns, constitute the framework of the layout – as with the streets of one of Vauban's fortified towns, or the city plans devised by Baroque architects like Bernini earlier in the seventeenth century.

The larger enclosed gardens of the Middle Ages, square or oblong in shape, often had perimeter paths of sand and gravel protected by a 'cloister' or tunnel-arbour built on wooden rods or

(Above) A giant urn silhouetted against the sky closes a vista at Chatsworth.
(Left) The laburnum walk at Bodnant, supported on a metal pergola frame.

withies and covered with roses, vines and ivy. These were intended to provide a walk in the shade, particularly for the ladies of the household at a time when the sexes were still very much separated in and outside the house, and when the palest complexions were also highly prized. In the early seventeenth century, Francis Bacon still recommends 'a Covert Alley, upon Carpenters Worke, about Twelve Foot in Height, by which you may goe in Shade, into the *Garden*' – and others framed 'likewise for Shelter, that when the Wind blows Sharpe, you may walke, as in a Gallery.'

The idea of the *allée* as an outdoor Long Gallery for exercise and conversation in fine weather can be confirmed by the number of such rooms whose barrel-vaulted ceilings are conversely decorated with plasterwork trellises of flowers, leaves and branches – a tradition carried right up to the twentieth century with Oliver Messel's trailing vines painted on the ceiling of the long gallery at Parham. Pleached lime trees were particularly favoured for walks from the sixteenth century 'for both shade and sweetness', as John Aubrey put it in his description of the Earl of Exeter's garden at Wimbledon. The scent of limes was balanced by their tendency to drop a black sticky honeydew on the innocent promenader, however, and other species such as beech and hornbeam also became popular – the former because it kept its leaf through the winter and helped preserve the 'architecture' of the garden from one season to another. Yew was of course even better for this purpose, and the tunnel of yew at Melbourne Hall in Derbyshire, planted by the Royal gardeners London and Wise about 1704 is – at just over 290 feet – thought to be the longest in Europe.

D'Argenville's *Theory and Practice of Gardening*, translated by John James in 1712, characterizes the different 'Palisades' or hedges lining an *allée* in highly architectural terms, 'making as it were a green Wall or green Tapestry'. The tallest, cut with the help of 'tall double Ladders and Rolling Carriages', he calls 'Fans and Curtains . . . which serve to stop the Sight, to shut up Places that are disagreeable, or to sever the parts of a Garden,' while 'those we call *Banquettes*, they are low Palisades Breast-high, ordinarily not exceeding 3 or 4 Foot.' Those most commonly found nowadays, clipped like boxes supported on stilt-like trunks – as in the stilt garden at Hidcote, or flanking the south garden at Chatsworth – he calls 'à l'Italienne', while the most elaborate of all 'cut into Arches', with 'Balls or Vases . . . formed by Shoots of Horn-beam . . . on the Head of each Peer . . . a Kind of Order of Rural Architecture.'

Elms were also used for the larger *allée*, such as the gigantic *patte-d'oie* or goose-foot pattern of three avenues radiating from a double semicircle of trees which was planted at Greenwich soon after the Restoration, probably following an original design by Le Nôtre. Though the great French garden designer never visited England, his influence was strongly felt, particularly after his master Claude Mollet's son, André, entered the service of Charles II. However, the idea of the 'limitless vista', created with ease in the flat landscape surrounding Versailles, was not so easily achieved among the highly compartmented small-holdings of Holland or the hilly countryside of much of Britain – and sometimes the effect had to be gained by painted 'Perspectives' or *trompes-l'oeil*, seeming to extend the vista into infinity. John Evelyn, who visited Saint-Germain in 1644, recorded that 'in the uper Walkes are two Perspectives very pretty ones, seeming to enlarge the allys,' and the painter Jacques Rousseau who worked in both France and England became a specialist in this field in the 1680s and '90s. D'Argenville describes a variation on the form with a false grotto opening, but calls such 'Perspective Works . . . now but little in use.'

The straight walk reached its apogee in the early eighteenth century, with elaborate stars of radiating vistas like those seen in Peter Rysbrack's paintings of Chiswick, or Balthasar Nebot's of Hartwell: each one aligned on a pavilion, an obelisk, a pillar, or an already existing 'object' at some distance. John Aislabie's principal avenue at Studley Royal was aligned on the towers of Ripon Minster; one of the Earl of Mar's *allées* at Alloa took in Stirling Castle, and another the Palace of Elphinstone; while at Easton Neston, Lord Lempster added a spire to the neighbouring church of Greens Norton, not out of solicitude for the parishioners or for the glory of God, but so that it would act as an 'eyecatcher' for one of his two principal vistas.

Many houses like Easton Neston, Erddig and Wimpole had a gallery on the upper floor running from front to back of the house on the central axis, offering views of several miles in each direction. Celia Fiennes, describing Ingestre in Staffordshire, records that 'the vista is quite through the house and so to the gardens and through a long walke of trees of a mile through the parke to a lodge or summer house at the end, which lookes very finely, it being a riseing ground up to the parke.'

Stephen Switzer was one of the first to express disquiet at the prevalence of the straight *allée* in his *Ichnographia Rustica* of 1718: '. . . tho' a few of these Walks are absolutely necessary, in Respect to the Grandeur and general Beauty of a Situation, as the Middle and Side Walk, and a very few Diagonals, yet it is an unpardonable Fault . . . to have scarce any Thing in a whole Design, but carries open Walks; so that . . . one shall scarce find any private or natural Turn in the Whole.' By contrast, he cites 'that beautiful Wood belonging to the Earl of *Carlisle*, at *Castle-Howard*, where Mr London design'd a Star, which would have Spoil'd the Wood; but that his Lordship's superlative Genius prevented it, and to the great Advancement of the Design, has given it that Labyrinth diverting Model we now see it.'

The privacy of 'solitary walks' like those in Wray Wood may seem a curious concept today, but the numbers of people attached to a noble household at the time meant that it would be difficult to see the length of a vista unencumbered by fellow humans. The garden as a place where man could commune with nature, already foreshadowed by the melancholy Elizabethan seeking 'the shade of the Greenwood tree', gained ground with the Natural Landscape movement. At the same time, writers like William Shenstone underlined the boredom of the long straight walk, compared with the serpentine path, revealing new Claudian 'pictures' at every turn: 'to move on continually and find no change of scene in the least attendant on our change of place, must give actual pain to a person of taste. For such an one to be condemned to pass along the famous vista from Moscow to Petersburg, or that other from Agra to Lahor in India, must be as disagreeable a sentence as to be condemned to labour at the gallies. I conceived some idea of the sensation he must feel, from walking but a few minutes, immured, betwixt Lord D—'s high-shorn yew-hedges; which run exactly parallel, at the distance of about ten feet; and are contrived perfectly to exclude all kind of objects whatsoever.'

Capability Brown's idea of a serpentine walk forming a circuit of the 'Pleasure Ground', either for walking or for driving in a pony trap, offered a very different kind of experience, although the viewpoints on the way were often contrived with just as much artifice. In the same way as it had become the common practice to taper a short avenue or *allée* so that it appeared longer than it was, Shenstone recommended a vista to be 'widened in front, and planted there with ewe trees, then firs, then with trees more and more shady, till they end in the almond-willow, or silver osier . . . which deception will be encreased, if the nearer dark trees, are proportionable and truly larger than those at the end.' Joseph Spence was also fully aware of the importance of perspective in 'composing' a picturesque view, and two of his 'general rules' about landscape design, written in the form of a letter to the Rev Mr Wheeler in 1751, propose how 'to make objects that are too near seem farther off: which is done by shewing more of the intermediate ground and narrowing your view to them more and more as it recedes from you;' while 'to draw distant objects nearer to you and make them seem part of your work . . . is done by hiding the intermediate length of ground and planting what may fall and unite, to the eye, with such distant objects.'

A garden building, or even the house itself, could provide such an 'object', varying greatly in appearance from whatever angle it was viewed. Thus the critical Polypthon in William Gilpin's *Dialogue upon the Gardens . . . at Stow* (1748), was finally persuaded to 'run out into the highest Encomiums of the many beautiful Terminations of the several Walks and Vistas; and observe how many Uses each Object served . . . "For Instance, says he, the pavilion you shewed me from the Temple of Venus, terminates that Terrace in a very grand Manner . . . Yet the same Building . . . view'd thro' a retired Vista, can take upon it the lowly Form of a close Retreat." '

The return of formal gardening in the nineteenth century brought with it a new appreciation of the straight vista, often arranged with steps so as to provide a higher vanishing-point, and thus an impression of greater length. At Biddulph Grange, the flights are arranged some way away from each other, but from the terrace in front of the house 'read' as one continuous stair of monumental proportions. The walk itself is lined with rhododendrons, first used for such a purpose by Capability Brown at Kew, and later increasingly popular planted under a canopy of taller trees. Other exotic shrubs like azaleas, Japanese maples and liquidambars gave colour to long woodland or valley walks, though there is the sad story of a whole walk of *Rhododendron campbelliae* being planted at Belvoir, without realizing that it would take fifteen years to flower – and being cut down in despair after fourteen years of patient waiting.

Towards the end of the century, the pergola walk came back into its own, reviving the old sixteenth-century idea of the tunnel-arbour but giving it a more architectural emphasis in keeping with the material used for the house, whether brick, stone or timber. Harold Peto's feeling for Italian Renaissance gardens led to pergolas of Doric or Ionic columns covered with vines, while Jekyll and Lutyens were content with the farmhouse character of rough-hewn stone or chalk pillars, supporting lichened oak beams, and covered with clematis and climbing roses. Thin metal pergola frames, first developed in Germany, were also used as a practically invisible support for tunnels of wisteria or laburnum – as at Bodnant – allowing the long clusters of flowers to hang down like bunches of grapes from a vine. At a time when country-house gardens are again being viewed as a series of 'outdoor rooms', these *allées* are reminders of the sixteenth-century long gallery or the seventeenth-century enfilade, though with a sense of controlled colour that owes much to twentieth-century interior decoration.

*P*ollarded limes in the French style lead to a flowery meadow at Cranborne Manor, Dorset.
(Left) The Ring Pond at Chatsworth, with the beech allée beyond, leading to a colossal bust of the
6th Duke of Devonshire, on a column made of blocks of marble from the Temple of Minerva Sunias. The serpentine
hedge was only eighteen inches high when it was planted in 1953, inspired by the 'crinkle-crankle' walls
sometimes found in old kitchen gardens, whose south-facing bays protected the tenderer plants.

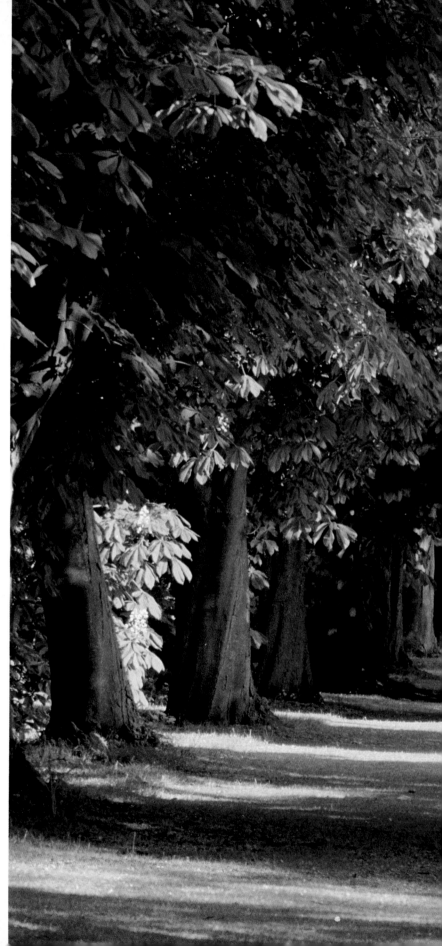

*T*he yew tunnel at Melbourne in Derbyshire, planted by
the Royal gardeners, George London and Henry Wise, about 1704 and – at
just over 290 feet – thought to be the longest in Europe.
(Right) One of the chestnut avenues at Anglesey Abbey, Cambridgeshire,
forming a cross-axis with the Great Avenue, planted to
commemorate the coronation of King George VI. The vast urn is one of
a pair, originally from Stafford House in London.

*T*wo hornbeam allées planted by Lawrence Johnston at Hidcote in Gloucestershire:
(above) the Long Walk, with its clipped hedges, given scale by the huge Monterey pine on the right;
(right) the Stilt Garden with its pleached 'boxes' – or 'palissades à l'Italienne' – supported
on trimmed trunks. As V. Sackville-West wrote, 'it gives a sudden little touch of France to this very
English garden'. The wrought-iron gate in the distance, flanked by evergreen oaks, frames
a wide view of the Cotswolds.

*V*istas prolonged by steps: (above) the long walk at Biddulph Grange, Cheshire, with flights placed at long intervals, but looking like a continuous staircase seen from the terrace of the house; (below) pots of marguerites guarding a brick stair at Sissinghurst; and (right) the axial walk at Knightshayes, parallel with the house. The steps and flanking stone figures mark the transition from formal to wild garden.

HERB AND KITCHEN GARDENS

The medicinal value of plants was one of the principal motives for gardening in the early Middle Ages, particularly among the monastic orders, which maintained physic gardens or herbariums on a large scale. However, the separation of utilitarian from decorative species was already a feature of Greek gardens in the first millennium BC, and the excavations at Pompeii show that the Romans had developed a thriving kitchen-garden tradition, which they brought north to the outer limits of the empire. Thus the elder Pliny's *Naturalis Historia* lists at least twelve different types of cabbage and kale, eleven types of lettuce, and numerous members of the onion family, while the Roman villa at Fishbourne in Sussex had a vegetable garden between its north and west wings, within easy range of the kitchen quarters.

(Above) The Herb Garden at Hardwick in Derbyshire, using mostly plants known before 1700. (Left) Fruit trees in blossom in the orchards at Penshurst Place, Kent.

The first English books on horticulture were largely devoted to the growing of vines, herbs and vegetables, like 'The Feate of Gardening' written in the 1330s by John Standerwyk, probably chief gardener to Edward III, which has long sections on the onion tribe, colewort, parsley and saffron, or the herbals of Friar Henry Daniel introducing rosemary (which had come to England with Queen Philippa of Hainault in 1340), and other foreign plants like germander and sweet marjoram, pomegranates and gourds. Gerard's *Herball* of 1597, perhaps the best-known and best-loved of all, was based on his experience as Lord Burghley's gardener at Theobalds and as curator of the garden kept by the College of Physicians in the City of London. His catalogue of his own garden at Holborn, published in 1596, includes the first printed reference to the potato, and the *Herball* was to influence and encourage botanists up to the time of Sir Joseph Banks.

Although the walled kitchen garden was conceived early on as a separate enclosure, herbs were often placed in the open knots of the Tudor and Stuart parterre. Gervase Markham in his essay 'Of Gardens' (1625) supposes the patterns to be set out in lines of rosemary, thyme or hyssop, and Bacon tells us that 'those which *Perfume* the Aire most delightfully, not *passed by* as the rest, but being *Trodon Upon* and *Crushed*, are Three: That is Burnet, Wilde-Time, and Water-Mints. Therefore, you are to set whole Allies of them to have the Pleasure, when you walke or tread.' At Sir John Danvers' house at Chelsea, the wide gravel walks nearest the house were bordered with hyssop backed by more than twenty-four varieties of thyme, and Aubrey records that 'Sir John was wont in fine faire mornings in the Summer to brush his Bever hatt on the Hysop and Thyme, which did perfume it with its naturall Essence: and would last a morning or longer.' Both fresh and dried herbs were also strewn on the floors of houses at this time to combat the less salubrious smells of a pre-sanitary age – just as they can be seen scattered in the path of Venus or Flora in Renaissance paintings.

Few Jacobean gardens were complete without vineyards or orchards. England had been so renowned for its dry white wines in the Middle Ages that they were exported in quantities to the Continent, and although the dissolution of the monasteries put paid to many of the finest growths, terraced vineyards were laid out on south-facing slopes at least as far north as the Trent. Robert Cecil's walled vineyard at Hatfield still survives, and his brother Lord Exeter had an equally large one in his garden at Wimbledon, drawn by Robert Smythson in 1609. John Rose, Charles II's gardener who appears in the famous picture attributed to Danckerts presenting the king with the

*A*pple-blossom time, (above) at Cranborne Manor, Dorset, and (below) at Penshurst Place in Kent, where the 'excellent fruit' was praised by John Evelyn as early as 1652. Orchards often occupied large sections of the kitchen garden, with wild flowers encouraged to grow in the long grass below the trees — only scythed once a year. (Left) A walk of cherry trees, underplanted with spring bulbs, leading down to the river Avon at Corsham Court in Wiltshire.

*T*he decorative value of common or garden vegetables
was realised in the seventeenth century, when formal potagers were laid out
under the influence of Louis XIV's gardener, Jean de la Quintinie.
A recent revival of the idea, with peas and beans, lettuces and cabbages,
marshalled in the mock-grandeur of a miniature parterre,
can be seen at Barnsley in Gloucestershire (above) and Tintinhull in
Somerset (below and right).

CANALS, CASCADES AND FOUNTAINS

S ince the walled oases of the ancient Arab world, water has been an essential adjunct of the garden, though its use grew out of purely practical needs. The narrow rill which is characteristic of the Moorish courtyard developed from irrigation channels; the fountain basin running with fresh water enabled camels and horses as well as humans to satisfy their needs more easily; while the pond or tank, stocked with fish, was an important source of food throughout the year, particularly employed by the monastic orders in northern Europe. The idea of the decorative canal, too, can be traced back to the defensive double moats of the Middle Ages, with the 'lists', where tournaments and jousts were held, lined with trees in between the two. This last development

(Above) The Water Garden at Blenheim, with Capability Brown's lake below.
(Left) The canal at Wrest Park, Bedfordshire.

came about in France only under the Valois, although the use of water for its purely pleasurable associations was already a feature of gardens in the ancient world. In Pliny's Tuscan Villa, the cold bath doubled up as a feature adorning the main terrace overlooked by the triclinium, so that from their couches the diners could see the water falling into the marble and hear the noise of the cascade.

Directly influenced by descriptions of such pleasure grounds, and by the excavation of Roman ruins including the Baths of Augustus and Caracalla, the architects of the Italian Renaissance revived the idea that gardens and buildings should be inter-penetrating spaces, with water as one of the main bonds between the two: the grotto and the nymphaeum, the fountain and the cascade, each in turn expressed the taming of one of nature's elemental forces by the hand of man. Elaborate waterworks and automata appealed to the scientifically inclined, and it was these which especially intrigued English visitors to Italy. Sir Henry Wotton, ambassador to Venice in 1604-12 and again in 1621-24, was delighted by a statue at Pratolino 'done by the famous hand of *Michael Angelo de Buonaroti*, in the figure of a sturdie *Woman*, *washing* and *winding* of linnen clothes; in which Acte, shee *wrings* out the water that made the *Fountaine*; which was a gracefull and naturall conceit in the Artificer'. At the same time he could appreciate the more abstract use of water as a decorative feature, for instance in a walk flanked by aqueducts, with little jets of water forming arches over it '. . . so as the *Beholder* . . . did walke as it were, under a continuall *bowre* or *Hemisphere* of water, without any drop falling on him'.

Another ambassador to Italy, Lord Lumley, who had gone as Elizabeth I's envoy to the Medici, erected fountains in her honour at Nonsuch, associating her with Diana ('Queen and huntress, chaste and fair', in Ben Jonson's words) and using water to suggest her purity. In one, a caryatid figure was seen through a veil of water; in another water gushed from the naked goddess' nipples; while a third consisted of a whole tableau in which Diana and her attendant nymphs, discovered bathing, sprayed Actaeon with water, causing antlers to grow on his head – with the result that he was devoured by his own hounds.

The prevalence of water in classical myth gave an opportunity to interpret such appropriate themes with a realism that could match any amount of carved wood, plasterwork, or tapestry inside the house. Here Ovid's *Metamorphoses* could come into their own at the turn of a stopcock, and the movement of fountains and cascades could provide the dramatic action in gardens that were increasingly seen in terms of stage sets and 'backdrops'. John Evelyn visiting Pratolino twenty-five years after Wotton found a 'Pan feeding his stock, the Water making a melodius sound through his pipe, & an Hercules whose Club yields a Showre of Water' – not to mention a grotto representing 'Vulcan & his family . . . with the huntings of Severall beasts, moving by the force of Water'.

The most famous of all such waterworks were at the Villa d'Este at Tivoli and the Villa Aldobrandini at Frascati, seen by almost every foreign visitor to Rome and imitated by innumerable English and French gardens of the late seventeenth century. Evelyn's description of Frascati seems to foreshadow the later doctrines of the 'Beautiful and the Sublime' (and the dawn of romanticism) with its account of 'a horrid Cascade seeming rather a greate River than a streame, precipitating into a large Theater of Water representing an exact & perfect Raine-bow when the sun shines out'. For the time being, however, it was the more artificial elements of the grotto with its 'hydraulic Organs & all sorts of singing birds moving, & chirping by force of the water, with severall other pageants and surprizing inventions', that were more popular with contemporaries.

Celia Fiennes describes the gilded lead fountain in the shape of a tree at Chatsworth, reconstructed in the nineteenth century but still able to give unwary visitors a soaking, and a clock in the garden at nearby Bretby 'which chimes the quarters, and when they please play Lilibolaro on the Chymes'. One of the earliest and most famous of such mechanical delights was the grotto at Enstone in Oxfordshire, created in the 1620s by the eccentric Thomas Bushell, previously a member of Francis Bacon's household. The 'Enstone Marvels', as they were called, particularly illustrated the connection between gardening and scientific advances at this period, with hydraulic effects like the silver ball rising and falling on a single jet of water, and optical experiments like the 'canopy of rain' formed to create a rainbow – in the manner of the Villa Aldobrandini. Bushell, described by a contemporary as 'a mad gim-crack yet hereditary to these Hermeticall and Proiecticall Undertakers', was also able to produce a wide variety of sounds from his waterworks, from 'the beating of a drum' to the 'chirping of a nightingale.'

Many of these ideas were also used by Isaac de Caus for Charles I and Queen Henrietta Maria (who visited the Enstone Marvels in 1635), and for the fourth Earl of Pembroke's celebrated gardens at Wilton. Here the little river Wylye was dammed to make one of the first cascades in England: a high waterfall with a curved lip once again employing the refraction of light to cause rainbows at certain times of the day. In hillier parts of the country, the French idea of a staircase of water was later adopted. That at Chatsworth was actually created by a Frenchman named Grillet in the 1690s, and, like the architecture of the house itself, was inspired by Louis XIV's Marly. A temple or cascade house, designed by Thomas Archer, was built at its head in 1711, with a fountain gushing from its cupola and spreading a film of water over the three tiers of the dome. From here, 'out of the mouths of beasts, pipes, urns, etc' in Defoe's words, 'a whole river descends the slope of a hill a quarter of a mile in length, over steps, with a terrible noise, and broken appearance'.

The cascade at Dyrham in Gloucestershire must have been equally dramatic, for Stephen Switzer records that 'the Weight of the Water, and the Falls are so great, that the Noise very near equals the Billows of a raging Sea, and may be heard at a very great Distance'. However, all that remains is the stone figure of Neptune at the top, striking the rock in vain with his 'exalted Trident'. The relationship between the internal architecture of the Baroque house and the 'outdoor rooms' of its surrounding gardens has already been suggested, and water was one of the chief means by which this was achieved. As well as the 'staircase' of water, there were the so-called *buffets d'eau* or tiered arrangements of fountains, imitating the sideboard of the state dining room with its brimming silver ewers, cisterns and wine-coolers. Above all, there was the long canal, equivalent to the enfilade or axial vista that was the hallmark of the Baroque interior.

While the interest in elaborate waterworks came from Italy by way of France, the idea of the canal and the technical development of dams, sluices and aqueducts used to bring water to the most unpromising terrain, came primarily from the Low Countries. William Blathwayt's hundred-yard-long canal at Dyrham, containing trout, perch and carp, as well as two tame swans, must have been influenced by his frequent visits to Holland as William III's Secretary-at-War. The Boeveys' canal at nearby Flaxley Abbey has been connected with their marriage into an Amsterdam merchant family, while another neighbour, Maynard Colchester of Westbury Court, had trading interests in Bristol which may explain the overwhelmingly Dutch character of his garden, with its three canals lined by yew hedges, restored by the National Trust in the 1970s. Whereas the canal was almost invariably placed on axis with the house in France, emphasizing the limitless vistas of Le Nôtre, those at Dyrham and Westbury were terminated by subsidiary buildings: in the first case an orangery, and in the second a tall gazebo like those seen in the paintings of Pieter de Hooch or Cornelis Troost – the ancestor of eighteenth-century fishing temples like that at Stoke-by-Nayland in Suffolk.

In the short-lived Baroque style that flourished under William and Mary and Queen Anne, the axial canal was occasionally favoured, as at Wrest Park in Bedfordshire (with Archer's domed temple at the end), at Easton Neston, or even at a comparatively small squire's house like Erddig in North Wales. By 1712, however, John James' translation of d'Argenville's *Theory and Practice of Gardening* was already proposing a canal on the cross-axis, some way from the house, large enough for a small flotilla of boats, and serving 'for an Inclosure to separate the Park and Garden'. The sides of these canals, like Charles Bridgeman's, may still have been straight-edged, with circular or octagonal basins at the ends (or in the centre) to give them variety, but it was only a matter of time before Hogarth's serpentine 'line of beauty' softened their contours and gave them the appearance of natural lakes. As with so many other advances towards the 'Picturesque', the catalyst was William Kent. In Horace Walpole's words, '. . . of all the beauties he added to the face of this beautiful country, none surpassed his management of water. Adieu to canals, circular basons, and cascades tumbling down marble steps, that last absurd magnificence of Italian and French villas . . . the gentle stream was taught to serpentize seemingly at its pleasure, and where discontinued by different levels, its course appeared to be concealed by thickets properly interspersed, and glittered again at a distance where it might be supposed naturally to arrive.'

If the canal was superseded by the lake, in imitation of Claude's ethereal visions, the cascade (in the old artificial meaning of the word) was replaced by the waterfall, in the manner of Ruysdael and Hobbema. Stephen Switzer had already praised the cascade at Dyrham for running 'not over polish'd Masonry, but over the roughest Frostwork and rugged Stone', while theorists like Roger de Piles, writing on landscape painting, had pointed to the future in their praise of rocks, '. . . of themselves gloomy, and only proper for solitudes; but . . . when they have waters, either proceeding from or washing them, they give an infinite pleasure, and seem to have a soul which animates them, and makes them sociable'. Almost Chinese in their attribution of human values to inanimate Nature, de Piles' theories reinforced the search for 'Sharawadgi' as Sir William Temple had called it, the idealization of nature within the microcosm of a man-made landscape. Kent's cascades in 'Venus' Vale' at Rousham, with their broad arches of rusticated rockwork, lead swans, and stone urns, may not seem 'natural' today, but in their sylvan setting they look forward to the more rugged waterfalls created by Capability Brown at Blenheim, and Charles Hamilton at Bowood.

Fountains too were to be condemned in the reaction against man-made contrivances. John Shebbeare's *Letters on the English Nation* written in 1755 in the guise of a mythical Italian visitor, 'Battista Angeloni', report that 'the *jet d'eau* is quite out of fashion in this kingdom . . . in truth, it is always unnatural to see water rising into the air, contrary to its original tendency.' But whereas the long canal and the stepped cascade were never to make a significant comeback in England, the fountain returned in the nineteenth century with the fashion for Italianate gardens, laid out along architectural lines. A favourite form was the triple-tiered *compotière*, found repeatedly in Victorian silver and ceramics, and ultimately deriving from the antique candelabrum rediscovered by Raphael and his contemporaries. But the single jet of majestic proportions, like Paxton's great 'Emperor Fountain' at Chatsworth, also told of new engineering skills brought by the Industrial Revolution.

The introduction of exotic water-loving plants – in which Paxton himself took a special interest – also created a demand for lily ponds. Bog gardens, like that at Sezincote, made by damming a small stream to make a chain of ponds, were equally popular, sometimes imitating the miniature river valleys of Japanese gardens. Towards the end of the nineteenth century, the publication of illustrated books on garden history also encouraged a return to the artificial water garden: Achille Duchêne's west parterre at Blenheim recalled the romance of Eugène Atget's photographs of Versailles; while Harold Peto's narrow rills, cut through the woods between the house and lake at Buscot, transposed the cooling channels of the sun-baked Alhambra to the damp and leafy landscape of rural Oxfordshire.

Water is still one of the essential elements of the country-house garden, and, like the use of glass in modern buildings, has come to be valued above all for its reflective powers. The round pond at Knightshayes, surrounded by a dark green wall of clipped yew planted in the 1930s, looks back to the mirror surfaces of the early-eighteenth-century Moon Ponds at Studley Royal, seen from the thickly-wooded hills above. Ben Nicholson's white marble 'wall' seen doubled in a still, black square of water in Sir Geoffrey Jellicoe's garden at Sutton Place, created in the 1980s, belongs to the same tradition: a return to the simple elements of the landscape garden – trees and grass, water and sky – unifying the works of man and nature in an ideal whole.

The Atlas Fountain at Castle Howard, acquired by the 7th Earl of Carlisle at the Great Exhibition in 1851, and installed in the centre of the south parterre by W.A. Nesfield.

*C*lassical reflections: (above) the Doric Temple at Barnsley in Gloucestershire, and (right) the
Pin Mill at Bodnant in North Wales. The latter, built about 1740 as a summerhouse at Woodchester, in
Gloucestershire, was acquired by the 2nd Lord Aberconway and moved to its present site in 1938.
It was he who also made the canal, on one of the five Italianate terraces below the house, with
spectacular views over the Conway valley to the peak of Snowdon.

LAKES AND
BRIDGES

But when the Lake shall these sweet Grounds adorn,
And bright expanding like the eye of Morn,
Reflect whate'er above its surface rise,
The Hills, the Rocks, the Woods, and varying Skies,
Then will the wild and beautiful combine,
And Taste and Beauty grace your whole Design.

Thus Lord Irwin was urged to improve his landscape at
Temple Newsam by the anonymous author of *The Rise and
Progress of the Present Taste in Planting Parks, Pleasure Grounds, Gardens,
Etc.*, published in 1767. The eighteenth-century passion for lakes,
sweeping away the narrow geometry of the long canal, was central
to the idea of picturesque gardening. But the technical knowl-

*(Left) The Palladian Bridge at Stourhead in Wiltshire, built by Henry Hoare
between 1760 and 1765. (Above) Swans on the lake at Osterley, Middlesex.*

143

edge that made it possible, the study of hydraulics, central to dam-building and the management of water-flow, was pioneered by the monks – particularly the Benedictines and Cistercians – of the Middle Ages. Their chains of stew-ponds stocked with fish, to be eaten on Fridays and other fast-days, as well as in Lent, are indeed the origin of several country-house lakes – like those at Nostell Priory and Woburn Abbey.

One of the first instances of a lake being excavated for purely pleasurable purposes in an English park (instead of being a fish tank or an adaptation of a defensive moat) was made in connection with the famous Elvetham entertainment given by Lord Hertford for Queen Elizabeth I in September 1591. Like so many other features of the Elizabethan garden this lake had an emblematic function, for it was laid out in the shape of a vast crescent moon, representing the Queen as the moon goddess, Cynthia, Diana or Belphoebe. Only three years after the defeat of the Spanish Armada, it particularly symbolized her role as mistress of the seas, for within it were three islands: one with trees cut like the masts of ships; another with a fort built by Neptune in defence of England; and a third with a mount twenty feet high, planted in ascending circles of privet, representing Spain – 'you ugly monster creeping from the South to spoyle these blessed fields of Albion'. In the firework display at the end of the evening, the monster was overcome by gunfire from Neptune's mount, anticipating the mock naval battles held on many lakes in the eighteenth century.

Roy Strong has traced the origin of such water festivals back to Charles IX's Fontainebleau and the entertainments held at Bayonne in connection with the treaty between France and Spain of 1565. Francis Bacon, who served in the English embassy in Paris in the following decade, may also have been inspired by French precedents in creating his ponds at Gorhambury, over four acres in extent. According to Aubrey, these were lined with coloured pebbles, while one of them had 'a curious banqueting-house of Roman architecture' on an island in the centre. Robert Cecil, Bacon's close friend, created a naturalistic river, crossed by several wooden bridges, immediately outside the garden at Theobalds, almost certainly inspired by Pliny's description of his layout at Tusculum – where the formal elements near the villa were deliberately contrasted with the informal beyond. But this has to be seen as a rare and isolated precursor of the eighteenth-century serpentine lake, planned to look like a majestic river winding through the landscape, rather than a static pond or reservoir.

In the Baroque period, large ponds were often created either to terminate canals or as independent features, though almost always of regular geometrical shape. As Batty Langley put it as late as 1728, 'the Circle, Elipsis, Octagon, and mix'd Figures composed of Geometrical Squares, Parallelograms, and Arches of Circles, make very beautiful Figures for Water . . . but of them all, the Circle is the most grand and beautiful'. The only irregular sheets of water were likely to be the reservoirs that fed the fountains, cascades and other waterworks, often placed at the furthest edge of the garden, and at the highest point. That at Dyrham, according to Switzer, took up 'near an Acre of Ground, and at the head is eighteen or twenty Foot deep; it has an Island in the Middle planted with Trees, contains Variety of the finest Water-Fowl, is well stock'd with most Sorts of Fish; and here you may sail in a Ship on a Mountain . . .'.

Elaborate duck decoys, like those shown in Kip's engraving of Haughton in Nottinghamshire, were often arranged on larger ponds of this kind, reflecting the same interest in natural history seen in Bogdany's contemporary paintings of wildfowl, and the popularity of aviaries as garden features. Visiting the lake at Wimborne St Giles in 1754, Bishop Pococke was shown 'a sea duck which lays in rabbits burrows, from which they are call'd Burrow ducks, & are something like the shell drake'. At Well Vale in Lincolnshire, the Muscovies that bred in profusion on the lakes above and below the house were so highly prized by their owner, Mr Bateman, that he adopted them for his family coat-of-arms in place of more conventional heraldic birds.

The shapes of lakes created in the picturesque landscape garden were largely dictated by the lie of the land, making use of valleys that already existed – even if vast teams of 'jocund labourers' were needed to make their outlines less regular, contributing an island here and a promontory there. Consequently, very few actually set out to copy an admired Old Master painting. The view over the lake to the pantheon at Stourhead is said to have been based on Claude's *Coast View of Delos with Aeneas* (now in the National Gallery in London); and at Castle Howard, Vanbrugh's lake and bridge, combined with a square building (the Temple of the Winds) and a round one (the Mausoleum), may have deliberately invoked the ingredients of other celebrated Claudes, like the *Pastoral Landscape with the Ponte Molle* (now in the Birmingham City Art Gallery). But on the whole it was the detailed treatment of smaller areas which were more likely to imitate the painter's brush, like parts of the lakeside at Painshill known to have been based on sketches by Salvator Rosa.

Sir William Chambers' account of Chinese gardening, published in 1757, stressed the infinite variety possible in the treatment of lakes and rivers – from the planting of reeds and weeping willows to the introduction of artificial rocks 'worn into irregular forms by the action of the waves . . . which they join with a bluish cement', and 'trunks of decayed trees, sometimes erect, and at other times lying on the ground, being very nice about their forms, and the colour of the bark and moss on them.' Above all, Chambers admired the way 'the termination of their lakes they always hide, leaving room for the imagination to work' – a cardinal rule of the later Picturesque landscape. As William Gilpin put it, in the 1790s, criticizing Capability Brown for failing 'more in river-making than in any of his attempts', '. . . an artificial lake has sometimes a good effect; but neither propriety, nor beauty can arise from it, unless the heads and extremities of it are perfectly well managed and concealed . . . you must always suppose it a portion of a larger piece of water'.

The bridge played an important part in such deceptions. Brown himself often used them to conceal dams, as at Wotton, where it came as a surprise to visitors to find the river at a higher level on one side than on the other; while at Kenwood the dummy bridge at the end of the lake is still no more than a wooden silhouette. At Kedleston, Robert Adam's three-arched bridge is combined with a spectacular cascade, an idea probably taken from the Falls of Terni which he had sketched during his time in Rome. Henry Wise's much earlier artificial river at Blenheim, one of the first in Britain, also fell in a cascade below Vanbrugh's monumental bridge. But later admirers of the Picturesque found their difference in scale absurd, and it was for this reason that Capability Brown was called in to flood the whole valley of the little stream known as the Glyme in 1764. The result, drowning not only the cascade, but many of the rooms which Vanbrugh had contrived within the piers of the bridge, was so spectacular that one can believe Brown's reputed boast on seeing the work completed: 'Thames, Thames, you will never forgive me'.

What contemporaries most criticized about Capability Brown's lakes was the comparative nakedness of their shores, perhaps implicit in Dr Johnson's remark to James Boswell when they visited Blenheim in 1776: 'You and I, Sir! have, I think, seen together the extremes of what can be seen in Britain: the wild rough island of Mull, and Blenheim Park.' But it is true that Brown was often dealing with flat countryside where the maximum of water needed to be seen from the house – unlike the Welsh border country, to which Payne Knight and Uvedale Price were accustomed, where raised viewpoints were normal, enabling lakes and rivers to be seen above riparian vegetation. William Shenstone, whose garden at the Leasowes also benefited from a hilly

*E*arly summer colour on the lake at Stourhead, with the Temple of Flora, built in 1744-46 and one of the earliest of Henry Hoare's garden buildings, on the right. Virgil's Aeneid provided the inspiration for many features of the garden, and the lake itself recalls Aeneas' vision of Father Tiber, while sleeping on the river bank, and his oath on waking: 'whatever spring may fill the pools which are your home, and wherever you yourself emerge in grandeur from the soil, always shall you be celebrated by me . . .'. The Temple itself bears the inscription 'Procul, o procul este profani' ('Begone, you who are uninitiated! Begone!'), the words spoken by the Cumaean Sybil before leading Aeneas into the underworld.

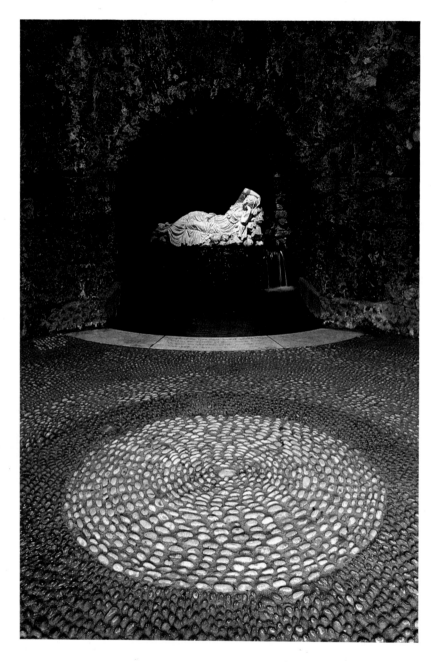

*T*he Nymph of the Grotto at Stourhead, evoking the cave in the haven near Carthage where Aeneas and his men took refuge from a storm. The grotto not only offered a view of the lake framed in the cave-mouth, but also contained a cold plunge. As Henry Hoare wrote in the hot summer of 1764, 'a souse in that delicious bath and grot, filld with fresh magic, is Asiatick luxury.'
(Right) The Palladian Bridge at Stowe, built before 1745, a combination of belvedere and eyecatcher, whose monumental proportions seem to enlarge the narrow stretch of water that it crosses.

*T*he bridge as garden ornament: (left) Vanbrugh's monumental arch at Blenheim — its lower rooms flooded when Capability Brown raised the level of the water; (above) Robert Adam's bridge at Kedleston, placed over the cascade between two lakes; and (below) the sweeping curves of Sir John Soane's bridge over the Ouse at Tyringham.

*A culmination of picturesque gardening: Sheffield Park in East Sussex. (Left) The falls
made by Pulham and Sons for the 3rd Earl of Sheffield in 1883; (above) the stone bridge between the
First and Second Lakes. The gardens were originally laid out by Capability Brown in the 1770s,
but with a wide variety of trees planted in the early years of this century, and
particularly chosen for their autumn colour.*

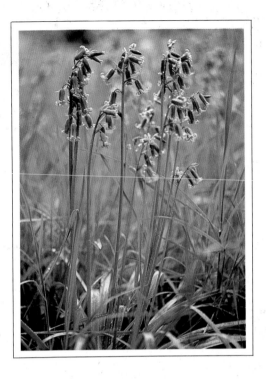

WILD GARDENS AND SHRUBBERIES

The idea of the wild garden or 'wilderness' developed from the sacred grove of trees, one of the oldest of all garden features since it dates back to the time of primitive man in the forest. Tree cults arose from the comparison of human life with the growth and death of trees – which the ancient Egyptians considered 'eternal souls'. The Greeks also believed in the mystical nature of the sacred grove, but at the same time gave it an intellectual basis: Plato's Academy was thus held in a plantation of olive trees, not only because they provided shade, but because their regular planting patterns were conducive to thought and contemplation. Teaching in the later Lyceum of Aristotle was actually peripatetic, conducted while walking along the tree-lined paths of the grove,

(Left) A woodland glade at Exbury in Hampshire. (Above) Bluebells in the long grass at Hever Castle, Kent.

and this concept of the wilderness as a place for intellectual pursuits was carried over into the gardens of seventeenth- and eighteenth-century England. Danckerts' picture of the Duke and Duchess of Lauderdale promenading in the Wilderness at Ham shows them accompanied by their chaplain with a book of sermons; Stephen Switzer records that the wilderness at Dyrham was 'a place for the sublimest Studies . . . and here are small Desks erected in Seats for that purpose'; while Bishop Pococke, who admired the woodland walks at Wimborne St Giles in the 1750s, noticed that 'in all the houses & seats are books in hanging Glass cases'.

Just as the Romans dedicated their groves to particular deities, so the *bosco* of the Italian Renaissance gave opportunities to interpret scenes from classical mythology. The story of Diana and Actaeon from Ovid's *Metamorphoses*, was a perennial favourite for its combination of woods and water, humans and animals, and the Grove of Diana at Nonsuch created by Lord Lumley as a tribute to Elizabeth I, may well have been based on gardens seen during his embassy to Florence in the 1560s. A German visitor, Paul Hentzner, described it in 1598 as 'a valley, thick set with pitch-trees and the sharp-pointed Cypress; by name Gargaphie, sacred to the active Diana'. The dark shades of this grove, beyond the formal parterres of the main garden, were intended to impart a feeling of pleasing melancholy – an attribute that was once again connected in the Elizabethan mind with imaginative and intellectual powers.

In the Middle Ages, the cold and dry qualitites of the melancholy humour were considered inimical to life, but Renaissance thinkers such as the Florentine humanist Marsilio Ficino resurrected the Aristotelian idea that such a temperament was a mark of genius. The title page of Burton's *Anatomy of Melancholy* (1612) shows the philosopher Democritus of Abdera seeking the shade of the greenwood tree, outside the bounds of a formal garden, while the same image can be found in Isaac Oliver's portraits of young gallants like Lord Herbert of Cherbury, brooding alone in naturalistic woodland settings. In Burton's words, 'what is more pleasant than to walk alone in some solitary grove betwixt Wood and Water, by a Brook side, to meditate upon some delightsome and plesant subject . . .'.

Francis Bacon visualized his ideal garden only four years later as having a '*Heath* or *Desart*' beyond the main parterres, which he wished 'to be framed as much as may be, to a *Natural Wildness*'. More in the nature of a shrubbery than a grove, it was to have '*Thickets*, made onely of *Sweet-Briar*, and honny-suckle, and some Wilde Vine amongst; And the Ground set with *Violets*, *Strawberries*, and *Prime-Roses* . . . here and there, not in

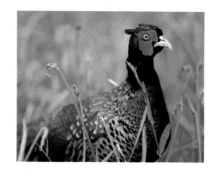

*H*ardy exotics in a woodland setting at Leonardslee, near Horsham in Sussex. (Above) A rhododendron in the Loderi Garden, named after famous rhododendron hybrids first raised here by Sir Edmund Loder. (Right) the Rock Garden, with azaleas, conifers, and trachycarpus palms.

*I*nformality in the 'jardin anglais': (above) the Medicean Lion at
Kedleston strolls through banks of rhododendrons; (below) spring wild flowers
on the terrace at Farnborough, Warwickshire; and (right) autumn crocus
at Tyninghame in East Lothian.

*T*he Nuttery at Sissinghurst Castle, Kent (left), fulfilling
V. Sackville-West's ideal of 'the strictest formality of design, with
the maximum informality in planting'. (Above) Leucojum at
Sissinghurst, and buttercups at Cranborne.

ORANGERIES AND CONSERVATORIES

A native of southern China, thought to have been introduced to the West by Marco Polo, the orange tree has been prized by English gardeners above almost any other fruit since the late sixteenth century. The orangery, the conservatory and the greenhouse – almost interchangeable terms throughout this period – were devised to conserve it and other tender 'greens' (such as bays, oleanders, myrtles, aloes and variegated hollies) during the harsh winter months, when they would otherwise have been killed by frost.

Elizabeth I's famous minister, William Cecil, Lord Burghley, may have been the first to grow oranges in this country, for in 1562 he wrote to a Mr Thomas Windebank in Paris asking him to

(Above) The interior of the conservatory at Syon, built in 1827-30.
(Right) Paxton's 'Conservative Wall' at Chatsworth, designed for camellias.

procure 'a lemon tree, a pomegranate and a myrt', as he already had an orange. He also asked for instructions as to the 'ordering' of his trees and was told to stand them in a sheltered position in the summer, and bring them into the house between September and April. Sir Francis Carew of Beddington in Surrey bought his orange trees from France in the same year, again through Windebank's agency, but according to Evelyn had them 'planted in the open ground and sheltered in winter by a tabernackle of boards warmed by means of stoves'.

One of the first records of a 'house for orange trees' can be found in the accounts of the King's Works for 1611-12, describing the garden at Somerset House in the Strand, laid out by Salomon de Caus for Anne of Denmark. An engraving in de Caus's book *Les Raisons des forces mouvantes* (1615) shows a walk lined with orange and lemon trees in tubs with a vault beneath in which they passed the winter, and this may perhaps illustrate the projected arrangement at Somerset House. André Mollet's layout at Wimbledon, made for another Queen, Henrietta Maria, in the 1640s, gave the 'Orange Garden' much more prominence – with a loggia on the east side of the house leading into a sunken parterre where the trees would stand at the corners of the knots during the summer, sheltered by the surrounding walls, and where there was a large 'Orange-House', with south-facing windows, where they could be stored in the winter. The inventory taken by the Parliamentarians when they took over the house in 1649 lists sixty trees, all in tubs, forty-eight of them laden with fruit, as well as six pomegranates and a lemon – valued at the enormous sum of £420.

The expense and rarity of orange trees continued to make them a symbol of prestige throughout the seventeenth and eighteenth centuries. Although Charles II's marriage to Catherine of Braganza encouraged their importation through Portugal, Nell Gwynn's role as the orange-seller was a much more rarefied occupation than might be imagined. The Dutch East India Company was another source after William and Mary's accession, when orange trees also became a sign of loyalty to the Whig cause and the House of Orange. Samuel Pepys was so fascinated by Lord Brooke's oranges at Hackney, which he saw in June 1666, that he 'pulled off a little one by stealth and eat it' – and it was to prevent similar pilfering that Lord Burlington's orangery at Chiswick was 'separated from the Lawn by a Faussee, to secure the Orange-trees from being injured by Persons who are admitted to walk in the Garden'. Here, according to Defoe, 'they are seen as perfectly, and when the Orange-trees are in Flower, the Scent is diffused over the whole Lawn to the House'.

A fantasy for an East India Company nabob: the conservatory wing at Sezincote in Gloucestershire, designed by S.P. Cockerell for his brother, Sir Charles, about 1805. The delicate Mogul ornament may be due to the artist Thomas Daniell, who assisted the architect, and whose knowledge of Indian buildings was unrivalled.

TEMPLES AND EYECATCHERS

There can be few countries in the world where the garden building has taken on more various forms, or had more different associations, than in Britain. Classical temples or Gothick ruins, Chinese pagodas or Moorish deercotes, hermitages and dairies, obelisks and arches, they are united only by the idea of 'Nature improved by Art'. This wish to introduce human scale into the unformed landscape of the wild goes back to a primitive fear of the unknown, still very much alive in the classical world where temples were built in remote and isolated places to placate the gods.

Few of these garden buildings had a strictly utilitarian origin, except for dovecotes, which were a valuable source of food in the

(Above) An obelisk at Bramham Park in Yorkshire.
(Right) Athenian Stuart's Triumphal Arch at Shugborough, begun in 1761.

Middle Ages. Like the one at Athelhampton in Dorset with over a thousand nesting holes, these became a symbol of seigneurial power, since they could be built only by lords of the manor – a restriction that existed in France up to the Revolution. They also produced excellent manure, and for this reason were usually placed near kitchen gardens or melon grounds. The usual round shape with a conical roof also had a strictly practical basis: an entrance for the birds being provided either through an open lantern, or through small dormers in the roof, while eggs could be easily collected from the pigeonholes inside by means of a revolving yard-arm, or potence.

It is tempting to associate the circular form of so many later garden buildings with the dovecote, but there was an equal incentive to provide an architectural contrast both with the house and the rectangular plots of the formal parterre, and it is this that more often explains the strange geometrical shapes (as well as the eccentric styles) of the later 'folly'. The circular domed arbours seen in illuminated medieval manuscripts and in the backgrounds of Elizabethan portraits were usually made of timber, used as a framework for pleached lime, beech or hornbeam: a type that was to remain fashionable right up to the early eighteenth century. Occasionally their interiors were also netted so as to form aviaries, and there is evidence that the remarkable wrought-iron arbour at Melbourne, made by the blacksmith Robert Bakewell in 1710 and exactly imitating the trellis arbours of an earlier date, may have performed a similar function.

This combination of the natural and artificial – a kind of growing architecture – reached its most remarkable expression at Cobham Hall in Kent, where in 1629 John Parkinson saw a large lime tree whose branches were trained to form no less than three arbours, one above the other, in each of which 'might bee placed halfe an hundred men at the least'. A staircase joined the three storeys, and there were floorboards on the different levels, Parkinson concluding that it was 'the goodliest spectacle mine eyes ever beheld for one tree to carry'. Many more of these elaborate tree-houses once existed, but one of the few to survive is that at Pitchford Hall in Shropshire, with a room high up in the branches probably constructed in the seventeenth century, and given charming rococo plasterwork decoration by Thomas Farnolls Pritchard in the 1760s.

In the Elizabethan and Jacobean period, no large garden was complete without at least one banqueting house, built very like the turrets on the roof of the great house and used for similar purposes. At Hardwick, five of the towers which give it its unforgettable silhouette were used for banqueting – that is to say for different dessert courses laid out so that the company could move from one to another by turn – and in the garden little pavilions of much the same form, with strapwork cresting and flat roofs, performed the same function in the far corners of the walled garden. Those at Montacute were built in the angles of the forecourt, and again designed by the master-mason William Arnold in the same style as the house, because they formed part of a unified architectural composition. At Blickling, however, Robert Lyminge's design for a banqueting house, made about 1620, is in a remarkable mock-medieval style deliberately contrasting with the up-to-date Renaissance ornament of the house. With its castellations and loopholes, it can be compared with some of Inigo Jones' designs for stage sets – and indeed garden buildings were often conceived as backdrops for the masques and outdoor entertainments of the time.

The free flow of air, said to dispel evil 'humours', was obviously valued in an age prone to disease, and this was one of the reasons for siting banqueting houses on the tops of hills. Here, too, they could offer a view over the knots of the formal garden, or provide 'stands' to watch stag-hunting, hawking, coursing or horse-racing in progress. The hunting tower at Chatsworth, probably designed by Robert Smythson in the 1580s, has rooms on four floors, all provided with chimneypieces for the benefit of the spectators, and even in the flat countryside of East Anglia, the octagonal gazebo at Melford Hall is raised up on a mound at the edge of the garden, overlooking the approaches to the house.

In the late seventeenth century the great territorial magnates were generally so engrossed with the building of their houses that they had little time for elaborate garden pavilions, and in any case the dominance of the Baroque house over its surroundings – an expression of absolutist power – was not to be prejudiced by any of its satellites. William Talman's design for a 'Trianon' for William III at Hampton Court was to be built on a new site across the river, outside the orbit of the Palace, and at Blenheim the only 'eyecatcher' of any significance was the Column of Victory at the end of the Grand Avenue.

The third Earl of Carlisle, creator of Castle Howard, was one of the first to change this state of affairs, building Vanbrugh's Temple of the Winds and Hawksmoor's Mausoleum before work on the house itself had been completed. A third important feature of the landscape was the pyramid, and it is particularly interesting to find the anonymous author of a poem on Castle Howard (possibly the Earl's daughter, Lady Irwin) writing in 1733 that 'Buildings the proper points of view adorn,/Of *Grecian*,

Roman and *Egyptian* form' – a passage which makes it almost certain that the different styles of the three buildings were deliberately chosen to represent the great civilizations of the past – with Vanbrugh's palace representing the Whig supremacy, greatest of them all.

The stylistic associations of garden buildings were taken a step further by William Kent at Rousham, for here all the ornaments within the garden were in the classical vein, and all those outside – the mill, the 'eyecatcher' and even the remodelled house – were in a picturesque Gothic. This emphasis on the idea of a classical Elysium, far removed from native traditions, was strengthened by the many allusions to the antique, from Venus's Vale to Praeneste, the seven-arched portico built above the Cherwell, its named derived from the Roman Temple of Fortuna Virilis at Praeneste (now Palestrina), famous for its gigantic terraces.

At Stowe, the plethora of garden buildings erected by Lord Cobham, as if to illustrate his family motto 'Templa Quam Dilecta' (How Beautiful are thy Temples), had a more overtly political message. Thus, the Temple of Ancient Virtue in the little valley known as the Elysian Fields, laid out 'after Mr Kent's notion' about 1735, was a domed rotunda of the noblest simplicity, based on antique Roman sources, while the Temple of Modern Virtue was a mock-ruin: a comment on the supposed immorality of Walpole's government, then in power. At the same time the Temple of British Worthies, celebrating patriots from King Alfred and the Black Prince to Queen Elizabeth I and Shakespeare, Milton and Locke, proclaimed the nationalist, anti-Gallican sentiments of Lord Cobham's own Whig faction. The message was equally clear in Gibbs' polygonal Gothic Building, dating from the 1740s, and summoning up ancient Saxon traditions of liberty and democracy.

The associational value of the Gothic made it a suitable style for garden buildings even when the inspiration was purely pictorial or literary. Roger de Piles' *Cours de Peinture* of 1708, widely known in England even before it was translated in 1743, commented that 'Buildings in general are a great ornament in landskip, even when they are *Gothick*, or appear partly inhabited, and partly ruinous: they raise the imagination by the use they are thought to be designed for; as appears from antient towers, which seem to have been the habitations of fairies, and are now retreats for shepherds and owls'. Vanbrugh was one of the first to argue for the retention of a genuine ruin in his unsuccessful plea to the Duchess of Marlborough to preserve the remains of Old Woodstock Manor at Blenheim: not only 'raise'd by One of the Bravest and Most

Warlike of the English Kings', but also 'One of the Most Agreable Objects that the best of Landskip Painters can invent'.

In much the same way, Pope wished Lord Digby to incorporate the ruins of Sherborne Castle in his landscape garden: 'the open Courts from building to building might be thrown into Octagons of Grass or flowers, and even in the gaming Rooms, you have fine trees grown, that might be made a natural Tapistry to the walls, & arch you over-head where time has uncovered them to the Sky. Little paths of earth, or Sand, might be made, up the half-tumbled walls . . . & Seats placd here and there, to enjoy those views, which are more romantick than Imagination can form them.' Near the entrance, he suggested that an obelisk might be erected with an inscription telling of the castle's ancient origins and its destruction in the Civil War, a history doing 'no small honour' to the owner's family.

The ruins of Halesowen Abbey seen from Shenstone's garden at the Leasowes, and, above all, the view of Fountains Abbey from John Aislabie's garden at Studley Royal, show how successfully such buildings could be incorporated into the eighteenth-century landscape garden. But few owners were fortunate enough to have the real thing, and most had to be content with artificial ruins like Sanderson Miller's castle at Hagley, which Horace Walpole praised as having 'the true rust of the Barons' Wars' – or his less 'finished' Gothic Tower at Wimpole. Lord Hardwicke seems to have planned the latter as a deliberate contrast to 'Athenian' Stuart's Prospect Room, for engravings of the two were sent to his friends with a letter in which he wrote 'perhaps the views may strike you as no bad contrast between ancient and modern times'.

Because garden buildings were often set in isolated positions, not intended to be seen at the same time as any of their companions (a rule particularly stressed by William Gilpin), they were freed from architectural restraint to an even greater degree than lodges, and were often of a highly experimental nature. Stuart's Temple of Theseus at Hagley, designed in 1758, was the first Greek Revival monument in northern Europe, while the giant Pineapple at Dunmore in Stirlingshire, built by an unknown architect in 1761, has to be among the oddest buildings in the world. Another Neo-classical prototype which was greatly admired was the so-called 'Tower of the Winds' at Athens, published in Stuart and Revett's *Antiquities of Athens*, and versions of this were built both at Shugborough in Staffordshire and Mount Stewart in Northern Ireland. Others conceived in a spirit of archaeological enquiry included a whole class of 'primitive' buildings, from Adam's thatched hermitage at Kedleston with its rough tree-trunk columns, to Thomas Wright's root house at Badminton with an interior of bark and moss.

Some garden pavilions were specially designed as settings for *fêtes champêtres* like Nicholas Revett's Music Temple (early on described as a 'theatre') on an island in the lake at West Wycombe. Occasionally a dairy also provided a backdrop for the 'simple life' of shepherds and shepherdesses, reminiscent of Marie Antoinette's *hameau* at Versailles. The tenth Earl of Exeter, who married a farmer's daughter known as the 'Cottage Countess' – and the 70-year-old Sir Harry Fetherstonhaugh of Uppark who married an 18-year-old dairymaid – both had charming tiled milking parlours constructed for their wives. But the finest were Henry Holland's at Broadlands and Woburn Abbey, respectively in the Gothic and Chinese styles, and both still stocked with their original Wedgwood creamware.

As well as model farms, many houses had aviaries or menageries – ancestors of the public zoological gardens of the nineteenth century. At Horton in Northamptonshire the Earl of Halifax's contained storks, raccoons, two young tigers and a bear, as well as rare birds and fish, while Thomas Wright's pavilion (which also served as a belvedere overlooking the park) was appropriately decorated with the signs of the Zodiac in the plasterwork cove, and 'four great Urns representing the animals of the four parts of the World' in the niches below.

Towards the end of the eighteenth century, the refinement of the principles of 'Picturesque taste' led to simpler buildings, playing a less dominant role in a wilder landscape. The influence of the old masters is clear in Walpole's breathless description of Hagley: 'there is a hermitage, so exactly like those in Sadeler's prints [after Paul Brill], on the brow of a shady mountain, stealing peeps into the glorious world below! and there is such a pretty well under a wood, like the Samaritan woman's in a picture of Nicolò Poussin! . . . that I wore out my eyes with gazing, my feet with climbing, and my tongue and my vocabulary with commending!' Thomas Whateley in his *Observations on Modern Gardening* of 1770 takes this a stage further in a passage probably attacking the famous hermitage at Hawkstone, where a resident 'friar' was kept to read visitors' palms or appear rapt in meditation: 'a hermitage is the habitation of a recluse; it should be distinguished by its solitude and its simplicity; but if it is filled with crucifixes, hour-glasses, beads, and every other trinket which can be thought of, the attention is diverted from enjoying the retreat to examining the particulars . . . though each be natural, the collection is artificial'.

It was in an effort to avoid the artificial that Repton and his contemporaries often preferred cottages or farm-houses to more elaborate garden buildings. The 'Red Book' for Blaise Castle (of 1795-96) illustrates a cottage on the edge of a wood in the main view from the house, with the explanation: 'a temple or a pavilion in such a situation would receive the light and . . . would not appear to be inhabited, while this, by its form, will mark its intention, and the occasional smoke from the chimney will not only produce that cheerful and varying motion which painting cannot express, but it will frequently happen in a summer's evening that the smoke from this cottage will spread a thin veil along the glen, and produce that vapoury repose over the opposite wood which painters often attempt to describe . . .'.

The 'Old Cheshire' cottage at Biddulph Grange, Prince Albert's Swiss chalet at Osborne, and the whimsy bargeboarded fantasies of architects like George Devey, continued this tradition into the Victorian period. But with elaborate formal gardens round the house replacing the landscaped park, there was little future for the temple and the 'eyecatcher' in the old sense of the word. Lord Berners' folly at Faringdon, designed by the Duke of Wellington in 1935 – a 140-foot tower with an arcaded look-out room at the top – or Raymond Erith's circular folly at Gatley in Herefordshire, built in 1964, show that the tradition is not entirely dead. Even now, some financier with the right mixture of eccentricity and affluence, will be considering a pepperpot of reconstituted stone on some nearby hill and (one hopes) remembering Payne Knight's words:

> . . . harsh and cold the builder's work appears,
> Till soften'd down by long revolving years;
> Till time and weather have conjointly spread
> Their mould'ring hues and mosses o'er its head.

*T*he Mausoleum and (left) the Pyramid at Castle Howard,
both designed by Nicholas Hawksmoor in the 1720s. Their Grecian and
Egyptian forms may have been deliberately chosen to complement
Vanbrugh's Roman Temple of the Winds – thus representing the three
great civilisations of the past.

*F*rom *'fêtes champêtres' to funerals: (left) Henry Flitcroft's Pantheon at Stourhead, seen across
the lake; (above) Sir John Vanbrugh's domed rotunda at Duncombe Park in Yorkshire; and (below) Joseph Bonomi's
mausoleum at Blickling in Norfolk, burial place of the earls of Buckinghamshire.*

*V*isions of Elysium: (above) the temple and obelisk in Lord Burlington's orange tree garden at Chiswick, (below) William Kent's Temple of British Worthies at Stowe, and (right) his seven-arched portico at Rousham, called Praeneste after the Roman temple at Palestrina. Dating from the 1720s and 1730s, such buildings were in the vanguard of the Palladian movement.

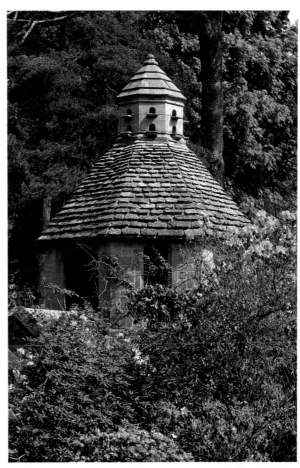

*D*ovecotes *may have inspired the circular garden buildings of later generations:*
(above) the stone-tiled pigeon house at Nymans, and the interior of a seventeenth-century
example at Rousham, showing the yard-arm used to reach the nesting boxes.
(Left) The dome of Robert Bakewell's wrought-iron arbour at Melbourne in Derbyshire.

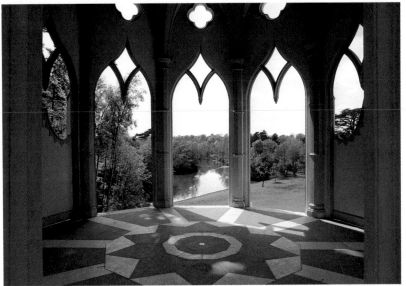

*T*he 'true rust of the Barons' Wars': (left) Sanderson Miller's ruined castle at Wimpole;
(above) Batty Langley's hexagon temple at Bramham; and (below) the view from Charles Hamilton's gothick
temple at Painshill in Surrey. The pleasing melancholy of mock-ruins, and the associational
value of the Gothic, as an expression of ancient liberties and national pride, made it a popular style for
garden buildings in the mid-eighteenth century.

*T*he variety of hard and soft woods found in Britain give its parks, in Walpole's
words, 'the richness of colouring so peculiar to our modern landscape':
(left) beeches at Bowood in Wiltshire; (above) silver birches at Thorp Perrow
in Yorkshire, and an ancient oak at Cholmondeley Castle, Cheshire.

*A*nimals as ornaments: (left) sheep in the park at Blenheim, (above) deer at Charlecote in Warwickshire, where Shakespeare is said to have been caught poaching; (below) pigs on the Home Farm at Shugborough, and a Highland bull at Tyninghame. The trimming of the lower branches by cattle was an important feature of the eighteenth-century landscape park.

Right: British gardens featured in this book open to the public

**Main map labels:**

SCOTLAND

Kinross
Tyninghame
GLASGOW
EDINBURGH
BERWICK
Floors Castle
Drumlanrig Castle
Cragside
NEWCASTLE
CARLISLE
Mount Stewart
ENGLAND
Holker Hall
Levens Hall
Thorp Perrow
SCARBOROUGH
Duncombe Park
Studley Royal
Castle Howard
ISLE OF MAN
YORK
Harewood House
Bramham Park
LEEDS
Temple Newsam House
HULL
Nostell Priory
ANGLESEY
MANCHESTER
LIVERPOOL
Tatton Park
SHEFFIELD
Plas Newydd
Bodnant
Biddulph Grange
Chatsworth
Penrhyn Castle
Cholmondeley Castle
Hardwick Hall
Erddig Park
Haddon Hall
Newstead Abbey
Chirk Castle
Alton Towers
Flintham Hall
Kedleston Hall
Wollaton Hall
Sudbury Hall
DERBY
Holkham Hall
Shugborough
Calke Abbey
Belvoir Castle
Grimsthorpe Castle
Blickling Hall
Powis Castle
Attingham Park
Melbourne Hall
NORWICH
LEICESTER
Burghley House
PETERBOROUGH
WALES
Hagley
BIRMINGHAM
Boughton House
Packwood House
Lamport Hall
Charlecote
Holdenby House
Castle Ashby
Anglesey Abbey
Farnborough Hall
Canons Ashby
CAMBRIDGE
IPSWICH
Hidcote Manor
Stowe
Wimpole Hall
Melford Hall
Sezincote
Rousham
Woburn Abbey
GLOUCESTER
Blenheim Palace
Waddesdon Manor
Wrest Park
Westbury Court
Ashridge Park
Cirencester Park
Hatfield House
OXFORD
Gorhambury
Barnsley Park
Nuneham Courtenay
LONDON
SWANSEA
Badminton House
Cliveden
Margam Abbbey
Blaise Castle
Bowood
CARDIFF
BRISTOL
Corsham Court
West Wycombe Park
Painshill
Dyrham Park
BATH
Cobham Hall
Buscot Park
Ashdown House
DOVER
Hestercombe
Stourhead
Heale House
Hever Castle
Penshurst Place
Tintinhull Manor
Wilton
Nymans
Scotney Castle
Sissinghurst Castle
Knightshayes
Montacute
Broadlands
Uppark
Leonardslee
Great Dixter
Cranborne Manor
SOUTH-AMPTON
Petworth House
Parham
Sheffield Park
Castle Drogo
EXETER
Exbury
Goodwood
BRIGHTON
PORTSMOUTH
Osborne
PLYMOUTH
Saltram House
ISLE OF WIGHT
PENZANCE

Dunrobin Castle
INVERNESS
Pitmedden
Craigievar
ABERDEEN
SCOTLAND
Crathes Castle
Blair Castle
Edzell Castle
Drummond Castle
PERTH

LONDON
Moor Park
Chiswick House
Kenwood
Richmond Palace
Kew Gardens
Osterley Park
Syon Park
Richmond Park, White Lodge
Ham House
Hampton Court Palace
Claremont